THE NIGHT GOD SHOWED UP

11 Life Lessons to Consider in Your Walk with God

TIM PATRICK

The Night God Showed Up
By Tim Patrick
Copyright ©2024 by Tim Patrick
All rights reserved.

No part of this book may be reproduced or transmitted in any form or by any means, electronic or mechanical, including photocopying, recording, or by any informational storage and retrieval system without written permission from the author, except for the inclusion of brief quotations in a review.

NO A.I. TRAINING: Without in any way limiting the author's exclusive rights under copyright, any use of this publication to "train" generative artificial intelligence (AI) technologies to generate text is expressly prohibited. The author reserves all rights to license uses of this work for generative AI training and development of machine learning language models.

ISBN-13: 9798323409389
V05202024
Also available in eBook

Edited by Sammie Barstow, sammiebarstow@gmail.com
Publishing Assistant: Ellen Sallas, TheAuthorsMentor.com

Contact the Author: timpatrick80@gmail.com

Unless otherwise indicated, Scripture quotations are from The Holy Bible, English Standard Version (ESV), Copyright @2001 by Crossway, a publishing ministry of Good News Publishers, Inc. Used by permission. All rights reserved.

PUBLISHED IN THE UNITED STATES OF AMERICA

THE NIGHT GOD SHOWED UP

11 Life Lessons to Consider in Your Walk with God

DEDICATION

This book is dedicated to the memory of our son, David. He and Erica served overseas for sixteen years before his passing. Their children, Elijah, Auburn Grace, and Evy, were born while they faithfully served our Heavenly Father in a closed country. They, like their Heavenly Father, had a heart for the nations (Is. 43:9). Erica, Elijah, Auburn Grace, and Evy currently serve in Taiwan.

On October 14, 2020, David moved from earth to Heaven. As he was exercising that morning, David's heart stopped beating and his earthly life ended. This happened just one week after a clear physical exam. You might ask, "How could this happen?" **Our times are in HIS hands.**

For parents who are raising young children, I must give a word of assurance. Judy and I never set out to raise a man of God and missionary. At times, we hung on for dear life.

Consider these examples. When David was a child, we had to seek professional counseling for him. He was so insecure that he could not face the anxiety of school without help. And then our Father gave him the gift of a godly wife, and they moved halfway around the world.

Another story comes from his junior high years. When he was 10-12 years old, he and a friend decided to run away from home (on a go-cart).

The final story occurred when David was sixteen. He wanted a car in the worst sort of way. I helped him get the car, a bright red Nissan. I have heard that bright-colored sports cars are a magnet for the police. Within two weeks he got two reckless driving speeding tickets. (It seems all teenage boys have a wild streak they must work through.)

And yet, the Lord brought this speed-loving boy up to be a man after His heart. It is to this incredible son, loving husband, intentional father, and faithful follower of Christ, David Heath Patrick, that I dedicate this book.

Side Note: As I write the pages of this book, I feel as if I am standing on David's shoulders. Do we miss him? Absolutely. There is not a day that passes that my wife Judy and I do not think of him. His life and death affected many. I do not say that because of sentimentality but as truth. His funeral was attended by hundreds of people and many more tuned into YouTube to listen to his funeral at a later date.

Would I like to have David back? Yes. As I go about everyday activities, I think how nice it would be to have David there, to share in the activity. Many times, he referred to us making "memories." David was one of the finest men I have ever met. He truly walked with God.

If the words of this book encourage someone in the faith or lead someone to faith in Christ, David's death will not have been in vain.

TABLE OF CONTENTS

PREFACE 1

Lesson 1 GOD SHOWS UP WHEN YOU NEED HIM MOST.............. 3

Lesson 2 YOU CAN BE ASSURED OF GOD'S REALITY 14

Lesson 3 GOD "REALLY" DOES SPEAK TO PEOPLE 22

Lesson 4 YOU CANNOT RUN FROM GOD.. 33

Lesson 5 GOD IS NOT FINISHED WITH YOU 38

Lesson 6 GOD SHOWS UP WHEN THINGS SEEM DARKEST......... 43

Lesson 7 DON'T QUIT WHEN THINGS GET TOUGH 52

Lesson 8 BELIEVERS SOMETIMES MAKE WRONG TURNS............ 58

Lesson 9 BELIEVERS SOMETIMES CRASH.. 67

Lesson 10 GOD'S AT WORK, EVEN WHEN HE SEEMS TO BE SILENT. 73

Lesson 11 GOD'S GRACE WILL CARRY YOU 89

PREFACE

The idea for this book began with a podcast. Some months ago, I listened to a podcast hosted by Carey Nieuwhof.[1] His guest that day was Richard Blackaby. On that podcast, Richard suggested that every pastor has at least one book hidden away in them. I owe Richard Blackaby, his words, and the Carey Nieuwhof podcast for motivating me to pen this book. The incentive for writing the book was the death of my forty-one-year-old son.

I wrote a book, *Carefronting People to Christ,* years ago. I had not planned to write another. Writing does not come easy. Every page is a struggle. Hopefully this book will spur someone to share ideas waiting to be birthed. In addition, my prayer is that it will encourage someone in their faith or bring them to profess faith in Christ.

---

[1] Careynieuwhof.com.cnlp554

The Pillar of cloud moved from before them
and stood behind them, coming between the
host of Egypt and the host of Israel.
And there was the cloud and the darkness.
And it lit up the night without one coming
near the other all night...
and the Lord drove the sea back
by a strong east wind
all night.
Exodus 14:20-21

Lesson 1

GOD SHOWS UP
WHEN YOU NEED HIM MOST

Have there been defining moments in your life that have affected the rest of your life? Defining moments stand out like mountain peaks. Such moments will grow your faith, and you will find an inner assurance you never knew until that point. Such experiences are not an everyday occurrence.

The defining moment I share gave me confidence and assurance that has followed me all my life. This moment became one of eleven lessons I share in the following pages. God used this event and these lessons to grow me. Hopefully my life testimony will encourage you.

Defining moments can show up in a time of innocence, or they can be profound mountaintop experiences you will never forget. Regardless of the occasion, defining moments are just that. They define who you are.

Before moving on, let me encourage you if you fall into the innocent category. What do I mean by innocent? Innocent spiritual experiences are those without fanfare. They are not dramatic. They are not published in books. In every church I have served there are people who feel as though they have nothing profound to offer. Most of the time these friends know they are saved, and they seek to honor God with their lives, but they cannot identify any mountaintop experiences.

Could I boldly say to you: that is simply not true. You are not an innocent spectator. You might not have experiences you would call mountaintop but take a deeper look.

You might not have experienced a life changing miraculous event that has everyone talking. You might not have experienced a dramatic moment that caused people to drop their jaw in awe. Every person, including you, is a walking miracle from God.

This book shares a defining moment that kept a young pastor from throwing in the towel and quitting the ministry. The mountaintop experience is unique to me; however, it is surrounded by ten life lessons that every believer should consider in their walk with God.

Every individual has unique experiences: birth, childhood, education, family of origin, and life lessons. The problem is that often we do not recognize these unique experiences until we look back. **This might indicate that you have a spiritual self-esteem problem. I say that gently because I have been there.**

Let's take Moses as an example. Moses was raised under the tutelage of Pharoah's daughter. No doubt God had his hand in Moses' upbringing. God miraculously protected Moses as a baby. I have questions about the circumstances surrounding Moses' floating in the Nile River. How did this transpire? Why did

Pharoah's daughter not see through this scheme? Why did she choose an Israelite to nurture Moses? There may be logical explanations to the events surrounding Moses' birth. I am not here to debate or discuss those explanations. The point I draw to your attention is that Moses was born like any other person. In his early years, he probably did not realize how unique his birth had been.

What is unique about your birth and early life? Your family of origin, parents, residence, and circumstances are unique to you. That is the special blueprint God has used to design you to be the unique individual you have become. That, dear friend, is not innocence. ***That is the sovereignty of God at work.***

Go back to the Moses story for a second look. Moses' early development was unique in two ways. His training was unique as a baby, as described in the previous paragraphs. In addition, his training was unique as an adult. In his early adult years, Moses was guilty of killing a man because of passion or anger or impulsiveness (Exo. 3). He did this to defend a fellow Israelite. Anxiety and danger resulting from this experience caused Moses to flee to the wilderness of Midian. This was the second aspect of Moses' training. He spent the next forty years living as a shepherd.

What training. Moses spent forty years learning the ways of Pharoah and forty years learning to be a shepherd and maneuver around a desert. When God needed a man to confront Pharoah, lead, and shepherd Israel from the land of Egypt, who was better prepared than Moses?

IF YOU THINK your story isn't noteworthy, think again. You are the unique person God designed you to be.

Sometimes the best training does not come from the classroom. Life experience is often the best training. Also, God's timetable is not the same as ours. Most seminary training lasts three or four years. Moses' training lasted eighty years. What if Moses naively thought he had nothing to offer?

In fact, in Exodus 3, Moses reflected an inferiority complex. Moses said to God: "Who am I that I should go to Pharaoh and bring the children of Israel out of Egypt?" (Exo. 3:11). If it was not for God providing Moses a qualified assistant, Aaron, who knows where this story would end?

If you think your story is not noteworthy, think again. You are unique. You are the unique person God designed you to be.

The Israelite story sets the background for my story. I too had a night experience with God. My experience was a life-defining moment. My experience seemed insignificant at first, but as time moved forward, I realized it was a mountain peak in my life. ***Sometimes the clearest view of life experiences is observed in the rear-view mirror.*** That was true for me.

Before sharing my story, we need to take a quick review of Moses and an incident from the life of the Israelites. For them, this was a night God showed up. **I am encouraged that God continues to give His people night experiences. He still shows up.**
In Genesis and Exodus, we discover God's relationship with the Israelite people. They were to become His chosen people. In Genesis, God established and identified Israel as His chosen people. Though Israel had a humble beginning, God promised Abraham they would eventually become "a great nation." As the story of Genesis unfolds, God develops His people. The stories of Abraham, Isaac, Jacob, and Joseph display God's hand at work creating a people for Himself.

God miraculously developed His people on history's stage. They were destined to be a blessing to the people of the world. Initially, Israel seemed to be an unstoppable force. Then disobedience and rebellion sidetracked them. As Genesis ends, the Israelite people find themselves in bondage in a foreign land, struggling under the iron fist of a leader named Pharoah. The Israelites had a pleasant experience under the hand of the first Pharoah they encountered. There were several dynasties of this family. The first Pharoah Israel met treated them with respect and showed favor toward them because of Joseph.

A later Pharoah was cruel and sought to snuff out the nation of Israel. About four centuries later, "there arose a new king over Egypt, who did not know Joseph" (Exo. 1:8). After Joseph, Israel spent 430 years living in bondage in Egypt.

God would not allow the Israelites to continue to remain in bondage and struggle. He sent Moses as a deliverer. Moses arrived on the stage of world history to lead the multitude of Israel out of Egypt. After winning a battle of wills with Pharoah, God prepared Israel to make the break and follow Moses from Egypt.

Initially, that experience went well. Following the sending of the ten plagues, Pharoah reluctantly agreed to allow Israel to leave Egypt and move toward the promised land. That process went well until Israel arrived at a huge turning point at the waters of the Red Sea. The Israelites faced the seemingly insurmountable waters of the Red Sea and the wrath of Pharoah. Pharoah had changed his mind and sent troops after the Israelites.
There were too many people to utilize a pontoon floatation across the Red Sea. The Israelites were stuck. They could not go back, nor could they move forward.

As noted, after Pharoah decided he was not pleased with the Israelites leaving, he pursued them with an army of soldiers and roared toward them with many horses and chariots. In that day and age, such a sight was sure to strike fear in the heart of any person. Israel trembled in fear and faced a second indomitable foe, Pharoah, and his war machine.

Before concluding the story of Israel and their encounter with Pharoah, please allow me to visit your heart. Do you need a miracle? Are you facing a seemingly insurmountable barrier? Always remember this word of assurance: God loves His people, and He shows up when they need Him most.

As Israel faced Pharoah one last time, they needed a miracle. They could visualize themselves as either being destroyed by Pharoah and his war machine or drowning in the Red Sea. There was no going back and moving forward seemed to be an impossibility.

To those of us who are thousands of years removed from this historical situation, it looks like an opportunity for God to show up and show out. That is exactly what He did (See Exo. 14:20-21).

Please note the scripture passage at the start of this chapter. Three times in just two verses reference is made to God showing up at night. I am not making an issue of night in a spiritual sense. In the Bible, night is a symbol for spiritual darkness, Satanic oppression, and rebellion against God. In this instance, however, night can be viewed as a reference to time itself. It happened that God showed up at night.

My own experience was a night visit from God. The name for this book comes from an experience when God's people, the Israelites, had a night visit from God. In no way do I seek to compare my story to that of the Israelites; however**, I am grateful the God of the Old Testament still works in our lives today.**

This incident occurred when I was a young pastor and had been serving for approximately ten years. I was tired, discouraged, and burned out. In addition to these emotions, which pastors encounter on a regular basis, I was hurt by the loss of a group of people from the church I was pastoring. The hurt was intensified by several people making disparaging remarks as they were transferring to another church. The disparaging remarks were painful, like salt being poured into a tender wound.

Discouragement, exhaustion, and burnout are powerful enemies, even without negative comments piled on top. I am thankful that God showed up and encouraged me on a Wednesday night after an evening worship service.

I was traveling by myself in rural Mississippi on a two-lane road when God spoke to my heart and encouraged me. I desperately needed a word from Him. I desperately needed Him to show up. I was nearing the point of giving up.

Sometimes when God speaks, I struggle to be sure it is God and not some wild emotion I am feeling. As God spoke, He said, "Tim, I have a lady I want you to help tonight." The words startled me and raised my curiosity. I owe the Lord an apology that I did not make a big deal of the event. Later, as I looked in the rear-view mirror of my life, I realized how significant that night was. I desperately needed God and He showed up. I praise Him for this life changing event, and gift.

A few minutes after the initial conversation, the story unfolded. I entered the interstate just south of Hattiesburg, Mississippi. After driving a few miles, I noticed a car on my side of the interstate moving along slowly without any headlights, just flashing warning lights. I drove up near the car and put my headlights on bright and shined them into the car. It was a lady. I discerned this was the person I was to help. I decided to pass the car and slow my speed. This anxious lady followed my unspoken lead. She followed me to Slidell. Then, when I thought she would leave the interstate and seek help, she did not. She continued to follow me toward New Orleans. I was headed to the New Orleans Baptist Theological Seminary located on the east side of New Orleans. When I reached the exit for the seminary I signaled and pulled from the interstate and into the seminary campus. I was surprised that the lady followed me.

When I stopped to get my room key for the night she passed by. This stirred my curiosity. I retrieved my key, jumped into my car, and went hunting for my travel friend. Near the back of the campus, I found her standing by a man I assumed to be her husband, on a sidewalk, telling her story. About an hour earlier, she had called her husband to explain that she was having electrical problems and asked him to pray.

It was about that time that God spoke to me, just outside Hattiesburg, Mississippi. and north of Slidell. As the lady and I related our stories, we celebrated God's work that Wednesday evening.

To illustrate how we overlook or minimize God's handiwork, consider these facts: Neither the lady nor I bothered to get each other's name or a point of contact. Back then, cell phones were unheard of. I did manage to record this event in my journal (see below). It is now 2023, and I started keeping a journal in 1984. The event occurred in 1986. I noted the event but did not overdramatize its importance in my life. I even called this event a "feeling," rather than a "word from God."

This event did, however, become a defining moment for me. I have told this story many times, reliving the experience. It became an anchor for me when I passed through other stormy days of my life.

Defining moments rise like mountain peaks from our lives and from those with whom we share. I never heard from the lady or her husband again. However, I have never forgotten the powerful experience of that evening. GOD SHOWED UP. It was a defining moment.

What did I gain from the experience?

I was reminded that, no matter how low you might get, God is always there. In Psalm 23 David said: "Even though I walk through the valley of the shadow of death, I will fear no evil, for You are with me" (Ps. 23:4).

I was reminded that, when you think there is nothing left on which to build, God is always ready to pick you up and move on. "Trust in the Lord forever, for the Lord God is an everlasting rock" (Is. 26:4).

I was reminded that when people get down on you, God is never down on you. My favorite character in the Bible is Simon Peter. Peter had the dubious distinction of being the disciple who denied Jesus three times as Jesus moved toward death on the cross. Yet it was also Peter who preached on the Day of Pentecost when three thousand people were saved. In addition, Peter contributed two books to our New Testament.

I was reminded that God is alive, active, and will be there for us no matter how bad the circumstances. People may criticize you, turn their backs on you, and doubt you. However, the God who called you is there for you. He has plans for you. When Israel was in bondage in Babylon, God said to them:

"For I know the plans I have for you, declares the Lord, plans for welfare and not for evil, to give you a future and a hope" (Jer. 29:10).

God will show up when you need Him most. Don't ever lose hope.

FOR REFLECTION

1. Read Exodus 14. Pay careful attention to verses 20-21.

2. What circumstances surrounded the Israelites as they stood before the waters of the Red Sea?

3. What was the condition of the Israelites?

4. When God showed up, what did he do for the Israelites?

5. Are there other stories/passages in the Bible when God showed up?

6. Do you need God to show up in your life?

Lesson 2

YOU CAN BE ASSURED OF GOD'S REALITY

The second lesson I learned occurred when God assured me of His reality. *He became real to me.* I have often pondered what causes faith to become real. It is not because of family. It is not because of knowledge. It is because God is working in your life. Paul said, "It is God who works in you, both to will and to work for his good pleasure" (Phil. 2:13).

What does it mean to be assured of God's reality?

It is that point in your life when you become sure of God's existence. You are sure that He answers prayer. You are sure that you have a personal relationship with Him. None of us feel we have mastered this phase of our spiritual lives. However, there is an inner confidence of the path we have walked with God.

In defining God's reality, words such as "authentic" or "genuine" come to mind. You will be confident that what you have is genuine.

Years ago, a gentleman from south Alabama, Ernest Dyess, spoke in a church where I served as pastor. Ernie, as we called him, came to discover the reality of God as a child. He wrote an interesting book, *God, If You're Real, Let the Cow Be in The Pen When I Get Home.* Ernie shares fifty-two heartwarming stories that relate God's reality. Ernie said he was in the process of discovering the reality of God when he failed to fulfill a responsibility when he was a boy. He had the responsibility of getting the family's milk cow in the lot in the afternoon. One afternoon he failed to fulfill this responsibility until it was late. As he rushed home he prayed a prayer, which became the title of this book. Ernie said the cow was in the lot when he got home.

For me there were three experiences that contributed to God's reality. **The first experience occurred when I asked Jesus Christ to enter my life and be my Savior and Lord.** My wife Judy and I both grew up in strong Christian families. In fact, both of our fathers were deacons in a Baptist church. Our mothers taught Sunday school and Vacation Bible School. Basically, our parents were at church every time the doors were open.

Faith is not passed down by proxy. It must become a reality in each person's life. Just because our parents were people of faith did not mean Judy and I were people of faith. When I experienced the miracle on the way to New Orleans, I had been a Christian for many years. Also, I had already learned many life lessons before that event.

I asked Jesus to enter my life when I was a ten- or eleven-year-old child. I cannot tell you the day, time, or date. I can only tell you my faith became real. My parents had shared the story of Jesus with me. My pastor had shared Jesus with me. Their sharing was for naught until I opened my heart by faith and asked Jesus to come into my life. This experience started me on a journey of following Jesus for almost sixty years.

There is a passage in John 9 when Jesus became real to a blind man. Jesus performed an unusual miracle by making a mud poultice and placing the mud on the man's eyes. Jesus instructed him to wash in the pool of Siloam. After Jesus healed the man, the Pharisees questioned whether this was in fact the same blind man the people of the community knew. I love the blind man's answer when the crowds asked him what had happened. The former blind man said, "One thing I do know, that though I was blind, now I see" (vs. 25).

> **AUTHENTIC FAITH** occurs because God is the one who initiates it.

Several truths from this passage can be helpful to those who are struggling to find reality in their faith. **First, faith begins and ends with Jesus**. It is not because of our denomination, our religion, or a religious tradition. It is a gift from Jesus. I had a rather non-dramatic encounter with Jesus. I was a naive child. Bells did not go off. Lights did not flash. My faith experience became real because Jesus spoke to me and changed my heart.

In addition to Jesus approaching me as he did the blind man, there were inner workings in my spiritual life. The first quality was God working to give me inner assurance. I put emphasize on the phrase "God working." Authentic faith occurs because God is the one who initiates faith. It does not come from religion, good works, a denomination, or a ritual. The blind man confessed: "One thing I do know, that though I was blind, now I see" (vs. 25). He found assurance because of his encounter with Jesus.

Many people struggle to find inner assurance. Several scriptures address this issue. John said: "I write these things to you who believe in the name of the Son of God, that you may *know* that you have eternal life" (1 Jn. 5:13). Paul said: "I am not ashamed, for I *know* whom I have believed, and I am convinced that he is able to guard until that day what has been entrusted to me" (2 Tim. 1:12).

My conversion to faith in Christ started my discovery of God's reality. However, there was a point in my life when I struggled to find inner assurance about my relationship with Jesus Christ. **This struggle was the second experience which contributed to God becoming real to me.** My salvation was not dramatic. There were no bells or whistles. After finishing seminary and while I was serving my first church, I struggled to find assurance about my personal relationship with God. I questioned God's reality in my life. My parents' faith did me no good at that point. My seminary training did me no good. My wife, as encouraging as she was, could not help me. I had to have a fresh encounter with Jesus Christ. Only Jesus can give inner assurance. I would not say such an experience is a second conversion experience. For some people, such an encounter may result in a true conversion experience. What they discover, however, is that they were not converted to faith in Christ the first time. They really are having a foundational conversion experience.

My wife, Judy, is a good example of this. She had a "seeming" conversion to Christ at the age of eight. She said she was following other children the night this occurred. You notice I used the word "seeming." Judy says she was not truly converted to faith in Christ. However, at the age of sixteen, Judy had a "true conversion" to Christ. She was convicted of her sins by the Holy Spirit. She repented of her sins and turned in faith to Christ. Judy testifies she has never doubted that experience. It was solid and real.

When I went through this experience of finding inner peace with Christ, a friend advised me to seek Jesus with all my heart. He advised me to consider a carpenter's square. He said to let one side of that square represent Jesus promises to me (John 3:16;

Romans 6:23; 10:9-10; etc.). The other side of the square was to represent my faith. My friend advised me to pray this prayer: "Jesus, I accept your promises by faith." He said once you have claimed Jesus' promises then let your faith stand strong. My friend advised me to tell Jesus, "If I go to Hell, it is because you have lied to me." The night I prayed that bold prayer God gave me inner assurance.

Before receiving inner assurance from God, I had to revisit the experience I had when I was ten or eleven. Jesus carried me back to my conversion experience. This fresh visit occurred when I was twenty-four, after I finished seminary. My conversion experience began at a Christian camp when I was ten or eleven years old. A camp counselor shared the Gospel with me. He shared John 3:16, Romans. 3:23, 6:23, and other passages of scripture. I prayed that bold prayer described on the previous page. *Jesus revealed to me that my faith was real. I did not need a new conversion experience.* That experience was dramatic. My conversion and the search for inner peace with Christ were two distinct experiences. They both contributed to the discovery of God's reality.

Many people go through this type of struggle. Some people discover they never were converted to faith in Christ. They are born again. For others, this evaluation and struggle with God reveals reality. They know they are saved and that Jesus lives in their hearts. There is nothing wrong with a sincere struggle to know God in a more intimate way.

The blind man we read about in John 9 found inner assurance. Next**, his faith became personal**. He said: "one thing I do know, that though I was blind now *I see*" (vs. 25). I discovered I could not enter Heaven because of the faith of my parents. The faith must be mine.

A third experience which contributed to the reality of God in my life occurred when I was sixteen. At the age of sixteen, I experienced God's call to the ministry. As I stated earlier, my parents went to church every time the doors were open. I have heard speakers testify that they were "drug" to church. That was true for me. As a sixteen-year-old, I was between my "real" conversion (at ten or eleven) and my search for inner assurance in my early twenties.

When I was sixteen, I accompanied my parents to a revival in our church. A young evangelist had been invited to preach a weekend revival. They thought he would be able to relate to the younger crowd. One night at the revival, he challenged the young people to seek God's will for their lives. The night I went to that revival I was not expecting to "run into God," but I did. This was the third significant experience that contributed to God's reality in my life. As I sat in that revival service, I was captivated by the young evangelist. He was passionate, entertaining, and challenging. He inspired me to go home and seek God's will for my life. When I shared this in a previous paragraph, I spoke in plural form. For me, that revival experience became personal. When God spoke to me, it was as if no one else was in the service.

I accepted his challenge. I went home that night and prayed a simple, naive prayer. It went something like this: "God, what do you want me to do with my life?" I was planning to go to college and get a degree in agriculture. As I prayed that prayer at the age of sixteen, God carried me back to a conversation that occurred about eight years earlier. When I was a child, six to eight years old, my grandfather made fun of me. He said I talked so much that I would someday become a preacher. My grandfather was not a man of God, but God used him as a spokesman to me.

This was fascinating. I had not remembered that conversation for eight or ten years. However, in that quiet moment at the age of sixteen, it was as if a video had replayed that conversation. This was a dramatic moment in my life.

Everyone is seeking to discover reality in their walk with God. I believe even non-believers would like to discover this truth.

Has there ever been a time when God became real to you? This reality could have been expressed in a dramatic event or an experience spread over a period of time. God's reality should be personal. God's reality should give you inner assurance. The greatest miracle is the miracle that occurs when God becomes real to you.

The reason I wrote this book was to encourage people in their faith walk. Your spiritual walk is more than a one-time experience. The experience in New Orleans was not the end of my faith experience.

FOR REFLECTION

1. Read John 9.

2. How did Jesus help make faith a reality for the blind man? How did the blind man confess and acknowledge the reality of Jesus?

3. Read Luke 2:8-20.

4. How did faith become a reality for the shepherds? How did Jesus' reality affect the shepherds?

5. Read Matt. 1:18-25.

6. How did faith become a reality for Mary and Joseph? How did the reality of faith affect Mary and Joseph?

7. At what point in your life did God become more than a concept? What effect did God's reality have on you? What events or experiences contributed to God's reality in your life?

Lesson 3

GOD "REALLY" DOES SPEAK TO PEOPLE

When God called me to serve in ministry, I learned a valuable lesson. *He really does speak to people.* In chapter 2, I referenced a dramatic call to ministry. During the night trip on the way to New Orleans, God clearly spoke to me.

Shortly after I submitted to God's call upon my life, I had an experience that moved me deeply. My pastor invited me to attend a ministers' retreat. At that retreat, an evangelist from Shreveport spoke. The evangelist related an experience he had a few days prior. He said he got up on a Sunday morning to speak at a local church. As he traveled, he related how the Lord impressed him to turn in to a particular parking lot. To make a long story short, the evangelist met a homeless man in the parking lot and led him to faith in Christ.

I felt challenged by that story. I recognized nothing of that nature had ever happened to me. However, I was motivated to seek the Lord and be more available as He speaks to me. I must admit, I have not always gotten it right when God spoke to me. At that retreat, I was introduced to a new and exciting lifestyle—hearing the voice of the Living God.

For many of you reading this book, God's speaking is a given. You accept God's speaking because you observe Him speaking to people throughout the Bible and you have experienced it. However, I have found God's speaking to be a mystery to many. I once had a prominent church leader confess to me: "I do not know if I can honestly say that God has spoken to me, outside of my conversion experience."

I made two observations as I considered that statement. First, many people confess that God spoke to them, resulting in their conversion to faith in Christ. After their conversion, there is often a disconnect. Those same people are like my friend. They cannot identify a time when God spoke to them.

God's voice is not an audible voice, but it is clear, nonetheless. I believe all people are looking for the reality that God speaks. That is the truth underlying the Bible. God spoke to mankind through a book. In that book, we find many occasions when God spoke. Consider:

- In Genesis 1, the Bible indicates God said/spoke at least ten times.
- In Genesis 3, when God related to Adam and Eve, He spoke to them.
- In Genesis 5, when the first murder occurred, God spoke to Cain.
- In Genesis 6-9, God spoke to Noah in His dealings with him.
- In Genesis 12, God spoke to Abram when He called him out of Haran.
- In Exodus 3, God spoke to Moses, when He called him. Not only did God call Moses but He spoke to him throughout his life.

- Throughout the Old Testament, God spoke to His workers: Joshua, Saul, David, Daniel, and the list goes on and on.
- In addition, God spoke to believers in the New Testament.
- Jesus spoke to the twelve disciples when He called them.
- Jesus spoke to Saul when he experienced a dramatic conversion (Acts 9).
- The Holy Spirit guided Paul as he made his missionary journeys.

There are many books, which discuss the reality of God speaking. It is not my purpose to do a comprehensive treatment of God's communication with us. I cover this truth because it is a very real part of my life.

I am often asked: how can you know when God is speaking to you? There is no definitive answer that is the same for everyone. God speaks to each person in a distinctive way.

> **GOD INITIATES** communication. We do not have to pander to or pester Him until He caves.

I have found helpful guidance from the life of Samuel. Samuel struggled to discover the reality of God's voice. He went from being a naive confused young man to being a leader of God's people. This is found in 1 Samuel 3.

Consider the lessons observed in Samuel's special encounter with God. First, Samuel learned that **God initiates communication.** It is nice that we do not have to pander or pester God until He caves in to us.

Jesus once told a story about an ungodly judge and a lady who approached him with a need. He said the lady went to the judge and pestered him about her need. She continued to pester the judge until he granted her request. Jesus' point is that God desires that His children persevere in prayer (Luke 18:1-8). This parable teaches us that God desires to hear our prayers.

In Samuel's case, he was in neutral gear preparing to go to sleep when God's messenger approached him. This encounter was not something for which Samuel was searching. He was not thinking about it or seeking it. God initiated the encounter.

This should ease the pressure we often feel as we consider God's communication with us. We should not feel pressured to be attentive listeners. We do not have to aggressively seek God. He desires to communicate with us. He initiates it.

Another lesson we learn from Samuel comes from his environment. **He heard God speak in the quiet of a bedroom.** The environment was not a crowded market. He was not pursuing God in a crowded church service. This is not to say that God is silent in church services. Some of God's clearest direction in my life (conversion, calling; etc.) occurred in a worship service through men of God. For Samuel, God spoke to him in the quietness of his bedroom.

When a couple needs to have an important conversation about a subject, they do not do so in public. They do not talk in the middle of a crowd. Can you imagine a couple trying to carry on a serious conversation at a football game?

> **A QUIET PLACE**
>
> in your home can facilitate "hearing" God.

Evangelical churches seek to instill a special discipline in believers to facilitate their growth. We call this a daily quiet time. It is a time when believers quietly read their Bibles, pray, and listen to God. The key word is the word "quiet." God does not delay speaking until we pursue Him or aggressively try to force him to speak with us. It is His desire to speak with us. He initiates, whether in a church service or in our bedroom. Point: he needs your undivided attention.

I have often used Jesus' example in Matthew 14 where we find the story of a busy day in Jesus' life. Jesus had performed many miracles, and the crowds were flocking to him. He was in a desolate place where there was no food to feed a hungry crowd of people. Jesus performed one of His greatest miracles when He took five loaves of bread and two fish and fed the crowd. From that miracle, the disciples gathered twelve baskets full of broken pieces of bread.

Jesus must have been tired from ministering to the pressing crowd. From there "after he had dismissed the crowds, he went up on the mountain by himself to pray. When evening came, he was there alone" (Matt. 14:23-24). Jesus refreshed himself and listened to His Father in a "quiet" place.

In following Jesus' example, we should have a quiet place where we go to be alone with God. The Bible says: "Be still and know that I am God" (Ps. 46:10). In Exodus 3, we read about the call experience of Moses. Moses was keeping the flock of his father-in-law in the wilderness of Midian. Moses was not actively seeking a word from God. However, God used the quiet location to speak with Moses.

This is a very important principle. As a rule, we will not hear God communicate while rushing about daily activities and fulfilling other duties. It is not that God cannot communicate with us. The fact is, we cannot discern His voice during a busy life.

Another lesson I observe in Samuel is that **God's voice is distinct**. When God spoke to Samuel, Samuel said "Here I am."

(1 Sam. 3:4). Initially, Samuel thought it was Eli speaking to him. However, as the experience unfolded, Eli helped confirm that God was speaking to the boy Samuel. This may sound like a shallow, simplistic answer, but the fact is true. When God speaks, you know it is God. It may take time to unravel and sort through what God is saying.

Down through the ages, the "called of God" knew God's voice to be God's voice. It may take the help of others, as Eli helped Samuel. However, God's voice is distinct. In your heart of hearts, you know it is God's voice. This is not something that can be taught. When God speaks you have an innate understanding that God is speaking.

God communicates by speaking but also through other means.

- In Genesis 18, God spoke to Abraham through three guests (angels).
- In Exodus 3, God spoke to Moses through a burning bush.
- In 1 Kings 19, God spoke to Elijah through a "low whisper."
- In Acts 10, God spoke to Peter in a vision of a sheet being lowered from Heaven.
- In Acts 9, God spoke to Paul by blinding him.

When I was in seminary, I had a unique experience of God communicating with me. Any student will always have the need for more income. Seminary students are no exception. I have always been a huge basketball fan. While in seminary, I decided to get trained as a basketball official and earn school money by calling basketball games. I started out good and got certified. However, after a few weeks I got the impression that I was not to officiate ball games.

One Monday afternoon, a friend and I were returning from North Louisiana. That night I was supposed to attend a basketball officials' meeting, as a part of our training. As we passed through Baton Rouge on our way to the seminary in New Orleans, our car developed a flat tire. I was distressed because the flat tire was forcing me into a time pinch in getting to the meeting. We got the tire changed and I watched my time. I realized I had time to make the meeting. When we arrived at the seminary, I rushed my things to the dorm and ran to the car. Another trial, I had no headlights. The failed headlights shot any possibility of making the meeting. By the way, the next morning the lights worked fine and never gave me another minute of trouble.

> **GOD WILL NOT STOP** speaking to you once He has started, and He will not treat it casually.

I asked the Lord what he was trying to teach me. The earlier impression I had, the flat tire and the failed headlights, seemed to veto the idea of me officiating basketball. God used these things to communicate with me. About two weeks after the Monday afternoon episode, I was called to serve as a pastor of my first church. I would not have the time to pastor, officiate basketball, and go to school.

Another lesson observed in Samuel's call **is persistence**. If God is speaking to you, he will not stop. Three times Samuel mistakenly goes to Eli asking what he (Eli) wanted to say. Eli instructed Samuel that he was not speaking. Finally, Eli discerned that God was speaking to Samuel so he said: "Go, lie down, and if He calls you, you shall say, 'Speak, Lord, for your servant hears'" (1 Sam. 3:9). God persistently spoke to Samuel.

I give this advice to parents of small children. Parents are often fearful of pushing their children into a premature decision to follow Christ. None of us would want this. I remind parents that God is persistent. If He is speaking to a small child about faith in Christ, He will not stop speaking. If the faith decision is an eternal decision, God will not treat it casually. He will continue to speak over a period of weeks and months. Parents can trust the God who created Heaven and earth. He will lead a small child consistently and persistently. That is a surefire way of knowing God is leading that child.

God called me to preach at the age of sixteen, but I did not submit to His calling until I was twenty-one. For five long years, God persisted in speaking to me. I am so grateful that God is persistent.

The Bible describes His longsuffering nature: "But you, O Lord, are a God merciful and gracious, slow to anger and abounding in steadfast love and faithfulness" (Ps. 86:15). Had it not been for God's persistence, I would have missed His will for my life. Once you discover God's voice and submit to it, He will open doors to confirm His calling upon your life. In short, God opens doors.

When I submitted to God's voice, my home church in Louisiana supported me. They paid for me to attend an international youth conference in Brussels, Belgium. Billy Graham preached a crusade in conjunction with this youth conference. God opened this door through my church family.

Another important principle in God's speaking is the **assistance of others.** When Samuel began to hear the voice of God, he was confused. He thought the voice he heard was Eli, the prophet of God. Samuel went to Eli three times before Eli surmised that Samuel was receiving a word from God. The important truth is that Eli was available to guide, comfort, and instruct young Samuel. Samuel did not have to sort through this experience on his own. He had a man of God to help him.

This same principle is true for us. God's people are there to assist when God speaks. I am reminded of the Apostle Paul's conversion experience (Acts 9:1-17). God sent a man named Ananias to guide Paul as he was sorting through God's words to him. Apparently, Ananias was an ordinary layman. However, God used this ordinary man to assist the greatest leader, apart from Jesus, in the New Testament.

Even so, God sends pastors, deacons, Sunday school teachers and believers to assist those who are sensing a word from God. You are not alone. God has people available to assist you in this important time.

A final principle from Samuel's life involves purpose. **God speaks to instruct, encourage, and affirm his servant (or servants).** In 1 Samuel 3, we find this illustrated in Samuel's life. "Samuel grew, and the Lord was with him and let none of his words fall to the ground." Samuel needed an affirming word from God.

Another life story illustrates this point. At one church I served, we faced a moral failure in a staff member. I had never faced a situation such as this. I went to the scripture for guidance. Galatians 6:1 says: "If anyone is caught in any transgression, you who are spiritual should restore him in a spirit of gentleness." I shared my findings with church leaders and suggested we should set up a restoration process. A restoration process in such situations is not practiced in most churches and denominations.

This proved to be a controversial subject. After a four- or five-step process the last step required a church vote. This process caused much discussion, and several people were upset. One church leader threatened to leave the church.

Five days before the vote, in my quiet time, I felt impressed to write the number 192 in my journal. I recorded the number on

Tuesday, April 6, at 8:30 P.M. I did not know what the number meant. The following Sunday, the affirmative vote was 192 in favor of the staff member. You can see the abbreviated journal entry below.

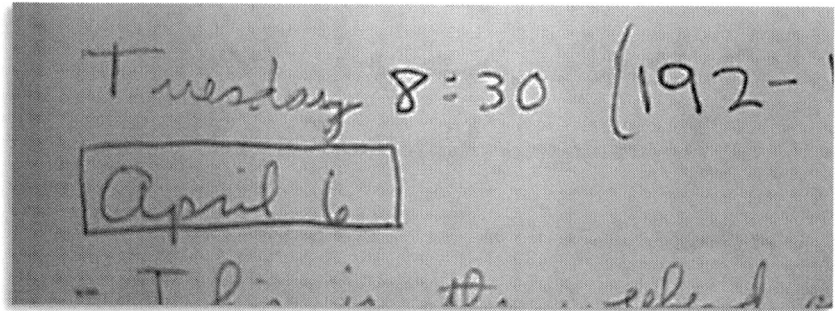

This four-month period was traumatic for me. My doctor had to place me on an anti-depressant during this period. I did not claim to be a prophet with a vision of the future. I did not stuff this in people's faces. I took this to be God speaking to a "green" pastor who was on the right track. Even so, Samuel was on the right track. God will come alongside his servants when they are uncertain about their next steps.

FOR REFLECTION

1. What experiences do you have when God spoke to you?

2. Study Acts 9:1-9. How did God speak to Paul to bring about his conversion to faith in Christ?

3. In Matt. 4:19, how did Jesus speak to His first disciples?

4. In Genesis 6, how did God speak to Noah about the events surrounding the flood?

Lesson 4

YOU CANNOT RUN FROM GOD

You would think the dramatic nature of my call experience (chapter 2) would have translated into obedience. For me, it did not.

I had a stubborn, rebellious heart when God called me into His ministry. That spirit was not appropriate. I had to be led beyond such an attitude. Put this idea in the context of your conversion. The Bible teaches that you enter the Christian life by being "born again."

This is like what happens when a baby is born. The baby is born into life. However, that baby must learn, grow, and develop. God does not miraculously change us into a fully developed follower at conversion. Some people do experience a dramatic conversion that radically changes their life, such as the conversion of Saul who later became the Apostle Paul (Acts 9:1ff). His conversion was dramatic. He was blinded as God captured his attention. Most people do not experience such a dramatic conversion.

At the age of sixteen, God called me into the ministry. My life, sadly speaking, represented a person who chose to run from God, much like Jonah. Jonah is the proverbial example of a person who sought to run from God. When God called him to preach in Nineveh, he ran the other direction.

> **YOU CAN'T OUTRUN GOD.**
>
> You will make yourself and everyone around you miserable if you try.

Why do people run from God? I had three reasons why I ran from God. **I ran from God because I was afraid**. I did not know what obedience would require of me. This was like Jonah's experience. He would not go to Ninevah to preach because he did not know what to expect from God.

Are you running from God? If so, you will think you can outrun Him. As a fellow traveler, let me share a word of advice. You cannot run from God. You will make yourself and everyone around you miserable.

Another reason I ran from God was related to the first: fear. I was afraid of what people would think of me. I was afraid what obedience would do to my relationship with others.

Also, I ran from God because I did not have a love relationship with Him. I was driven by tradition, religion, and guilt. God needed to lead me to a point where joyful obedience was the driving force in my life.

God used a young lady named Cindy toward this end. When I met Cindy, I was running from God. I was miserable. At that point, I was more attracted by hormones than God's Spirit. Cindy was a bubbly, enthusiastic teenager. More than that, she was excited about her faith.

Cindy and I spent time doing things teenagers enjoy. We water skied, rode horses, attended movies, played games, and the like. However, there was one huge difference. She was sold out to God and enthusiastic about her faith. I endured her church activities and youth Bible studies.

My life began to make a U-turn one night at the conclusion of a teen Bible study. After the study, I revealed to Cindy that I was running from God. She was kind and supportive and did not preach to me. However, a few days later she dropped a bombshell. She told me God had revealed to her that we should stop dating. I had never heard such language in my life.

It was not that other people refrained from such language. Such language was not in my vocabulary or a part of my heart language. Cindy's revelation broke my heart. It was not the loss of a girlfriend, but the subtle message God was communicating to me: "You cannot run from God."

The night Cindy broke up with me, I cried like a baby on my way home. After five years of misery, in fighting against God's call on my life, I was nearing a turning point of submission.

After several months of wrestling with God, He brought Cindy back into my life. We started dating again. On our first date, she asked how I was doing. I revealed to her I was ready to submit to God's will for my life. Cindy and her youth leaders rejoiced at my good news. After dating Cindy for a few weeks, the tables turned. One night I shared with Cindy that God gave me a revelation like her original revelation. I told her God had revealed to me that we should no longer date.

This break-up experience taught me two amazing lessons. *First, it reinforced the truth that God really does communicate with His children.* My call experience started me down this path. As I started down the path, I discovered that God does reveal himself and communicate with His children. He will communicate with His children, even about girlfriends and significant relationships.

This was all new for Tim Patrick. My faith became more than a ritual or tradition. My faith became a living reality. I could have added this story to chapter two when I discussed God's reality. God's reality should permeate every area of our lives.

The second lesson I learned from this breakup experience was the joy of obedience. When I was living in disobedience, there was no joy. I was miserable. I thought I could orchestrate joy apart from God's will.

The night I revealed to Cindy what I perceived to be God's will about our relationship, I was filled with inexpressible joy. That night, instead of crying on the way home, I sang. Believe me, I am not a singer. However, when you seek to obey God, joy flows from your heart. Nehemiah once stated: "the joy of the Lord, is our strength" (Neh. 8:10).

As I lived through the girlfriend experience, I was amazed at the change that came over me. It was not me but God in Christ working in me. I discovered that being an obedient follower of Christ was not so bad, after all.

FOR REFLECTION

1. Has there ever been a time in your life when you attempted to run from God (conversion; calling; morality issue)?

2. How did it feel when you attempted to run from God?

3. How did God move you through it?

4. Read the book of Jonah.

5. How did God start out communicating with Jonah?

6. What do you notice about Jonah's rebellion?

7. What do you notice about God's discipline of Jonah?

Lesson 5

GOD IS NOT FINISHED WITH YOU

God showed up in the car on the way to New Orleans. Had you judged my spiritual life by that experience, you would have given me high marks in spiritual maturity. Sure, this was a spiritual mountain peak for me. However, I did not reach that peak overnight. It was the culmination of many lessons learned in prior years. It also was the prelude to many lessons learned since that day. What is the point? Growth takes time, and it must fall into God's timetable. In short, God is not finished with us, and it is an ongoing process.

Recently, I noticed an advertisement in a Christian Book Distributors newsletter (September/October 2023). Max Lucado has written a new book entitled *God Never Gives Up on You*. Max does an uplifting retelling of the story of Jacob. He explains how God led Jacob despite his many failures.

As I write this book, I am approaching seventy. Some of the events described in this book were not pleasant. Some of you have walked through far worse trials.

GROWTH TAKES TIME

It is an important reminder that growth takes time and trials are spread over the scattered years of our lives. Our impatient response might be, "God, let's get over this. Teach me what you want me to know and let's move on."

> and trials are spread over the scattered years of our lives.

Thankfully, God patiently works with us to reveal His ways and plans. He did this in the Bible. Much of the Bible was revealed through progressive revelation. The arrival of Jesus clarified many lessons about God and other spiritual truth. However, it took men a while to comprehend the truth God was revealing to them.

Sometimes I feel as if I made a failing grade in faith. God has been working on me for seventy years. Sometimes I feel as if I take one step forward and two steps back.

Growth comes by way of trials, and it takes time. However, God continues to nudge us toward spiritual maturity. Let's take Simon Peter as an example. Simon Peter became the leader of the disciples and a key spokesman for the early church. Those were amazing accomplishments. To me, the amazing thing about Peter's life is that he gave his life as a martyr for Christ. He did not decide to be a martyr. Jesus spent years working with him and growing him.

Consider Peter's development. His growth in faith was like a roller coaster ride. We first met Peter in John 1. His brother, Andrew, introduced him to Jesus. Jesus saw the potential in Peter. The word "Simon" conveyed the idea of Peter's impulsive nature. Peter tended to be impulsive and struggled with foot-in-mouth syndrome.

Peter starts off well. He is willing to leave his fishing trade and follow Jesus. Not long after starting his discipleship journey, he triumphantly proclaims Jesus to be "the Christ, the Son of the living God" (Matt. 16:16). No one had ever spoken such words before. He got an A in discipleship 101.

In this same conversation, Peter stuck his foot in his mouth. He rebuked Jesus when Jesus announced He was headed to a cross. Peter said, "Far be it from you, Lord, this shall never happen to you" (Matt. 16:22). He went from a spiritual mountain peak to a dark night of the soul. Jesus said to him: "Get behind me, Satan. You are a hindrance to me. For you are not setting your mind on the things of God, but on the things of man" (Matt. 16:23). Talk about a pendulum swing. The pendulum continued to swing. Six days later, Peter experienced another painful lesson in growth. Jesus took Peter, James, and John "up a high mountain" for the transfiguration. Jesus' desire was to underscore the truth of His identity.

As they arrived on the mountain, Moses and Elijah appear and talk with Jesus. Peter was struck by this episode and made what he considered to be a profound statement. He says "Lord, it is good that we are here. If you wish, I will make three tents here, one for you and one for Moses and one for Elijah" (Matt. 17:4). Peter's declaration was commendable.

However, he missed the significance in his declaration. He was equating Jesus to Moses and Elijah. Moses and Elijah were two of the greatest men in Old Testament days. However, Moses and Elijah were not the Son of God, who would die for the sins of mankind.

God's desire was for Peter, James, and John to understand that Jesus was "my beloved Son" (Matt. 17:5). When God thundered his disapproval with Peter's statement, Peter took a new step of faith.

Peter had gotten it wrong. Only time and falling could move Peter in the right direction.

One further lesson from Peter's life illustrates the value of time and trials. Peter had the dubious distinction of being the only disciple who denied Jesus three times. This occurred after Jesus warned him it would happen. Peter boldly predicted this would not happen. Peter said, "Even if I must die with you, I will not deny you" (Matt. 26:35). Peter was guilty of three verbal denials of Jesus. Finally, he failed the absence test. He was not there when Jesus hung on the cross.

In no way do my trials compare to those of Peter. What is the point? We might have a mountaintop experience "when God shows up." That is not the end. God is still working on us. He is not finished.

FOR REFLECTION

1. As you read the previous description of Peter's spiritual pilgrimage, what stands out to you?

2. Read the following passages from Peter's life. Would you describe each as going forward or going backwards?

   Matt. 4:19
   Matt. 16:16-18
   Matt. 16:21-23
   Matt. 17:1-8
   Matt. 26:30-35; 40
   Matt. 26:69-75
   John 21:1-19
   Acts 2:1-41

3. Take a few minutes to draw a spiritual timeline of your life. Mark the highs and lows and how you perceive each event. Take time to share with someone else about your journey.

4. What has been the most impactful event in your lifetime, on your spiritual life?

Lesson 6

GOD SHOWS UP WHEN THINGS SEEM DARKEST

Do you ever feel as if trials converge in your life? When trials are many, we can understand and sympathize with Job. He was faithful and offers an example of a man who walked with God. More important than Job's faithfulness was God's faithfulness.

When trials show up, God displays His love and faithfulness. We cannot predict when, how, and where He will show his hand, but be assured He will. The Apostle Paul said, "Faithful is He who called you, who also will do it" (I Th. 5:24).

Lamentations also discusses this principle. Jeremiah lamented: "He has driven and brought me into darkness without any light" (3:2). Additionally, he says: "My soul continually remembers it and is bowed down within me" (3:20). Jeremiah felt the difficulty of his trials. However, he shares one of the most beautiful words of hope in the Bible. "The steadfast love of the Lord never ceases; his mercies never come to an end; they are new every morning; great is your faithfulness. The Lord is my portion, says my soul, therefore I will hope in him" (3:22-24). The old saying, "It is darkest just before the dawn," is a good commentary on this principle.

My trials were not of the magnitude and nature of Job's. However, I share this chapter because the night God showed up was mixed among the trials our family faced.

> **WHEN TRIALS SHOW UP,** we cannot predict when, how, and where God will show His hand, but be assured He will.

When I was in seminary, I once heard a lady share a testimony I have never forgotten. This testimony was shared at a Wednesday night, student-led chapel service.

The discussion that night focused on God's involvement in our trials. The Bible says: "We rejoice in our sufferings, knowing that suffering produces endurance, and endurance produces character, and character hope, and hope does not put us to shame" (Rom. 5:2-5).

The seminary student discussed the many trials her family was facing. She discussed financial hardship, health issues with a child, and the challenges of church work. As she concluded her testimony, she said: "We have been praying that God will take away our trials and give us better days." She said: "My husband and I agreed, why are we praying for God to take away the trials? Trials are the very thing God is using to grow and teach us." WOW.

I could relate to her testimony. Two of the most challenging years of my life were mid-1984 to mid-1986. This stands out because I started keeping a journal in 1984. And the New Orleans event was in July 1986. I mention a few trials our family faced during these two years. The convergence of these trials highlights the marvelous grace of God that will keep you from falling. This time, for me, illustrates how God shows up when things seem darkest.

One of the key trials I faced would not be recognized by most. It is recognized mostly by pastors. **I was caught up in the numbers game**. When I first went to the church I was serving at the time, it was in a slump. There had been tension surrounding the previous pastor's leaving. It often takes time to move a church out of such a slump. Each week I recorded in my journal the attendance from that week. I would record statements like this: "attendance was up today"; "attendance was terrible today." During my tenure, that church experienced some of the best attendance ever. That led to celebration with the people, but it creates a false idol. The numbers game can be gratifying but a terrible taskmaster.

Another trial was **Judy's depression.** I will discuss it further in chapter 12. Judy is a walking miracle. However, it is important to include it in this discussion to contextualize how trials can converge. At one point during these two years, Judy had to drop out of church due to her depression. I had to do most of the shopping, childcare, and a lot of the housework.

At one point during this period, Judy worked in a daycare. She was committed to being a stay-at-home mom, however, financial trials necessitated that she work. At one point, the owner of the daycare privately shared with me that she might have to release Judy. Judy's depression and anxiety were sensed by the children. For us, the fear of losing this job was not good news. We already had financial issues.

Financial pressure was another source of trial. In addition to monthly expenses and routine financial issues that young families face, I found out I owed the Internal Revenue Service $600. That might not seem like much to most people. However, when you have been married for only six years and have two preschool children, $600 seems like a million. This also was in the mid 80's. Money would not go as far as it does today.

While I am discussing money, this is a good place to share how God showed up to meet the financial trial. Judy had taken a part-time job in a daycare. This helped our situation but did not cover the need. As a result, I was considering a part-time job. One day, out of the clear blue, a man showed up at our door. He was our rural mail carrier. He asked if I would be interested in a part-time job. I had not filled out applications or pursued a part-time job. He just showed up.

He asked if I would be interested in serving as his substitute mail carrier. Mail jobs are good jobs and pay well. Naturally I was interested, and God provided for a financial need. **God shows up when we need him the most**.

Another trial we faced was the result of a **car wreck**. My brother, Gary, and his family were in a head-on collision near Natchez, Mississippi. They were transported to a hospital in Jackson. I was the first family member at the hospital. I was alone when the Emergency Room doctor shared the unfortunate news that Gary would probably never walk again. Talk about feeling lonely. In addition, Gary's wife had a broken neck and had to wear a brace for several months. Her condition rendered her incapable of helping Gary in the rehab process.

Gary's rehabilitation was challenging for our entire family. At the time, I lived in central Mississippi. It was about a four-hour drive to the rehab hospital. This trial lasted several months until we felt some relief.

Another trial, during this two-year period came **from an individual in my church**. He was angry and often let his anger out on others. I and the church felt this tension. In fact, I once heard him threaten to strike another church member with a chair during a meeting.

This individual would criticize me and other church leaders and cause tension in church business meetings. He sought to undermine my leadership. During this period, our family lived in a church-owned home. We were required to pay our monthly electrical bill. At one point, our church treasurer shared with me that this man was inquiring if I was paying my electrical bill. Talk about trust. Each time this man caused a flareup I would go to his home and try to reason with him. I saw myself as a peacemaker. Most of the time after those visits, I felt as if I had accomplished something. Surprise, surprise. I was fooled. I spent several years agonizing over this individual. His flareups did not ease the burdens I felt in other areas.

Another trial came at the hands of **disgruntled church members**. In any church, there are always disgruntled people who are considering something better. People are always looking for a better preacher, better music, better fellowship, and the latest church "God is blessing."

For us, there was a church down the road that was growing by leaps and bounds. Our church was growing but not exponentially like this one. A group of our people started attending this church. There were 20-30 people in this disgruntled group.

This kind of experience is difficult on a pastor. Feelings of inferiority, jealousy, anger, and other emotions accompany such an experience. There is usually nothing you can do about such things; however, it will keep you awake at night.

I visited one of the couples from the group and tried to reason with them before they left. They used comments such as: "their worship is awesome"; "their fellowship is welcoming"; and "their preaching is wonderful." The straw that broke the camel's back, as the saying goes, was this: "Pastor, you are liberal." I could have bitten a nail in two, with that comment.

On top of these six trials, **I enrolled in seminary to begin work toward a doctoral degree.** That educational work was both good and bad. It was good in that it helped me move beyond burnout. I discussed the burnout in chapter six. It also brought a freshness to my heart.

The educational work was bad in two ways. First, it added to our financial burden. Second, it added to time pressures. The addition of this educational work brought me to a breaking point.

It was during this period when "God Showed Up." On one of my trips to the seminary in New Orleans, God showed up and inspired me to help the woman (chapter 1) on the interstate. I was at a dark spot in my life. When God inspired that event, it gave me new assurance, courage, and fortitude. That event has been a comfort to me for the past thirty-seven (plus) years.

There are several passages in the Bible when God showed up during times of difficulty. I am reminded of Acts 16. Paul had a vision of a man from Macedonia appealing for him to "Come over to Macedonia and help us" (Acts 16:9). Paul immediately went to Macedonia and found a receptive group by a river in Philippi.

From there, Paul moved to "the place of prayer" (Acts 16:16). It is human nature to think that when God inspires something, everything will go smoothly. While ministering at the house of prayer, Paul met a slave girl whose owners were profiting from her misfortune. This girl had a spirit of divination and practiced fortune telling. She followed Paul and Silas and cried out: "These men are servants of the Most High God, who proclaim to you the way of salvation" (Acts 16:17). This practice continued for several days. Finally, Paul expelled the evil spirit from the girl.

The slave girl's owners stirred dissension and spread lies among the crowd. This resulted in Paul and Silas being beaten and thrown into prison and labeled as being troublemakers. Things turned dark on the ministry of Paul and Silas. They were thrown into prison and their feet were fastened in stocks.

> **THE GREATEST EXAMPLE OF GOD SHOWING UP** occurred when Jesus hung on the cross.

Things seemed bleak for Paul and Silas. About midnight, Paul and Silas were singing when God showed up. God sent an earthquake and shook the foundations of the prison. The bonds of the prisoners were unfastened and many went free. Paul and Silas did not take advantage of that opportunity. They stayed and shared Christ with the jailer. He and his family came to faith in Christ.

The greatest example of God showing up occurred when Jesus hung on the cross. Jesus came to earth to display God's love for mankind. Jesus submissively moved through the pain and agony leading up to the cross, only to hang on the cross and feel as if God had deserted him. The human and divine side of Jesus played a game of tug of war. Finally, in desperation, as He hung on the cross, He cried "Eli, Eli, lema sabachthani? That is, "My God, My God, why have you forsaken me" (Matt. 27:46).

Even before Jesus died, some of the skeptics said: "He trusts in God; let God deliver him now, if he desires him. For he said, 'I am the Son of God'" (Matt. 27:43). The question among the crowd was "Has God forsaken His Son?" (Matt. 27:43).

Some bystanders thought Jesus was calling for Elijah. One person filled a sponge with sour wine and offered it to Jesus. At that point, "Jesus cried out again with a loud voice and yielded up his spirit" (Matt. 27:50).

I think it is important that we affirm the truth of what happened to Jesus. It was imperative that Jesus feel the agony of the cross to bear the burden of our sins. Feeling forsaken by His Father underscores the agony of that experience. However, it is imperative that we highlight God's plans. God planned to show up. After three days, Jesus rose from the grave. At the darkest moment in history, God gave mankind hope. Jesus' resurrection gave mankind hope that there is hope beyond dark days.

FOR REFLECTION

1. Has there ever been a time when you felt as if God deserted you?

2. Read Matt. 27:32-28:10.

3. What part does Jesus' play when we feel forsaken by God?

4. When you and I feel deserted by God, where does faith play into that?

5. The man who wrote a big portion of the New Testament, Paul, suffered horrible persecution and trials. Read 2 Corinthians.

Lesson 7

DON'T QUIT
WHEN THINGS GET TOUGH

Edgar Albert Guest wrote a poem that has been an encouragement to me and thousands of others.

> When things go wrong, as they sometimes will, when the road you're trudging seems all uphill, when the funds are low and the debts are high, and you want to smile but you have to sigh, when care is pressing you down a bit - rest if you must, but don't you quit.
>
> Life is queer with its twists and turns. As everyone of us sometimes learns. And many a fellow turns about when he might have won had he stuck it out. Don't give up though the pace seems slow - you may succeed with another blow. Often the goal is nearer than it seems to a faint and faltering man;
>
> Often the struggler has given up when he might have captured the victor's cup. And he learned too late

when the night came down, how close he was to the golden crown.

Success is failure turned inside out - the silver tint of the clouds of doubt, and when you never can tell how close you are, it may be near when it seems afar; so, stick to the fight when you're hardest hit - it's when things seem worst, you must not quit.

The Bible has much to say about persevering. This is true in passages of the Bible but also in the lives of biblical characters. Consider these passages. In Ephesians 6:10-18, we find Paul's directions about putting on the spiritual armor. To encourage perseverance, Paul closes this passage with an injunction. He tells us to "keep alert with all perseverance, making supplication for all the saints" (Eph. 6:18).

> **PERSEVERANCE REQUIRES FAITH**
>
> but it also requires faithfulness.

You would think that, if we have equipped ourselves with the armor of God, we would persevere. That is not the case. We must persevere in the use of the armor.

In 1 Cor. 15, Paul devotes himself to a discussion of the resurrection. There is no greater chapter in the Bible. What great news. Jesus Christ is the basis of our hope. However, Paul closes the chapter with a call to persevere. "Therefore, my beloved brothers, be steadfast, immovable, always abounding in the work of the Lord, knowing that in the Lord your labor is not in vain." (I Cor. 15:58).

Two of my favorite Bible characters display a spirit of tenacity. One of these characters has been used extensively in this book. Peter got it wrong on the Mount of Transfiguration. Peter got it wrong when he denied Jesus three times. Peter got it wrong when he was not present for the death of Jesus. However, Peter preached on the day of Pentecost when the church was established, and three thousand new believers came to Christ. Peter later wrote two books in our New Testament. Peter, with God's help, did not quit.

I once taught 2 Corinthians to a group of ministers. We thoroughly examined Paul's trials. Depending on how you name and count them, Paul mentions some twenty to twenty-five trials he faced. This could have been a list of ways to persecute a believer. WOW. Talk about tenacity and faithfulness. Paul once said: "It is required of stewards that they be found faithful" (1 Cor. 4:2). As he neared the end of life, he said: "For I am already being poured out as a drink offering, and the time of my departure has come. I have fought the good fight, I have finished the race, I have kept the faith" (1 Tim. 4:6-8).

As a pastor, I struggled with depression, discouragement, and burnout on a regular basis. Notice the following journal entries. The first journal entry was from 1997. The second was from 1999. At the end of each year I would go back and review my year: its challenges, triumphs, and trials. You can see, serving in ministry requires a "don't quit attitude."

Perseverance requires faith, but it also requires faithfulness. *It is more important that God has a hold of you, than you have a hold on God.* Hebrews 11 is called the "faith chapter." This chapter highlights numerous saints who persevered through the ages. They did not have an easy life. However, God had his hand on them.

And what more shall I say? For time would fail me to tell of Gideon, Barak, Samson, Jepthah, of David and Samuel and the prophets who through faith conquered kingdoms, enforced justice, obtained promises, stopped the mouths of lions, quenched the power of fire, escaped the edge of the sword, were made strong out of weakness, became mighty in war, put foreign armies to flight. Women received back their dead by resurrection. Some were tortured, refusing to accept release, so that they might rise again to a better life. Others suffered mocking and flogging, and even chains and imprisonment. They were stoned, they were sawn in two, they were killed with the sword. They went about in skins of sheep and goats, destitute, afflicted, mistreated—of whom the world was not worthy—wandering about in deserts and mountains, and in dens and caves of the earth. And all these, though commended through their faith, did not receive what was promised, since God had provided something better for us, that apart from us they should not be made perfect" (Heb. 11:32-40).

These saints clung to God's promises. They were faithful. That is a central teaching of Hebrew 11. They did not quit.

In Matthew 10, we find Jesus' words as He warned His disciples that they would face persecution. "Beware of men, for they will deliver you over to courts and flog you in their synagogues, and you will be dragged before governors and kings for my sake, to bear witness before them and the Gentiles." (Matt. 10:17-19). The disciples faced a challenging life. Sometimes they stumbled. Sometimes their fear and timidity got the best of them. When Jesus hung on the cross, most of them were not present. However, they persevered and, according to legend, ten of them faced a martyr's death.

FOR REFLECTION

1. Read 1 Kings 19:1-18.

2. How does it affect you that Elijah would move through such an emotional crash?

3. Why does Paul encourage perseverance at the conclusion of I Cor. 15, in verse 58?

4. How do you label this experience in Elijah's life?

5. When John Mark deserted Paul and Timothy (Acts 16:36-41), what may have caused this? Was Mark finished after this episode?

6. Read 2 Cor. 11:16-33. How many trials does Paul indicate he faced?

Lesson 8

BELIEVERS SOMETIMES MAKE WRONG TURNS

Have you ever made a wrong turn? On a recent hiking trip in the Smoky Mountains, I made a wrong turn. I was on my way to meet my son John at a trailhead in the Smokies. I was running close, because of time. I came to an intersection in the road. I was supposed to turn right but I got confused and turned left. You do not stop, put your car in reverse, and correct your mistake when you are on a busy tourist road. As a result, I had to go around a two- or three-mile road loop and go back down the mountain. Understand, I am mission driven when behind the wheel of a car. You arrive on time, or ahead of time, and delays, either unplanned or those of your passengers, are a challenge.

I had to retrace my steps. I impatiently and hurriedly rushed down the mountain. I finally regained the original intersection where all this began. The second go-round, I made the right turn and arrived at my destination.

Your spiritual life will involve missed turns. Some of the wrong turns may cause you to feel as though you missed God.

THE CHRISTIAN'S LIFE

is reflected in a combination of God moments and human moments.

A Christian's life will be a combination of God moments mixed with human moments. The night God showed up was a God moment. An experience from my early twenties illustrates a human moment when I made a wrong turn.

During the God moments, you know God is in control. In Psalm 23 David said: "Though I walk through the valley of the shadow of death, I will fear no evil; for You are with me" (v.4). In the human moments (wrong turns) you're not sure what is going on.

At the time of this human moment. I was the pastor of a church in rural Mississippi. Our church was involved with other churches in our area, being inspired by a world mission conference. We had several missionaries from around the world sharing their mission stories in our churches. Mission conferences are inspiring events that touch the core of your heart. This conference did that for me.

One night during the conference I felt a nudging of God at my heart about missions. I had never experienced a call to missions, but I felt an overwhelming tugging of my heart to submit to being a missionary. I shared this feeling with Judy, and she listened with supportive understanding. Judy was supportive but confessed that she had never felt called to be a missionary. I did not put her down nor did she me. We agreed to pray and seek the Lord in this matter.

As time drifted by, I felt this tugging on several other occasions. I recorded these tuggings for a number of years. I did not go looking for such a call. It was not some emotional feeling. I genuinely felt God had called me to be a missionary.

I have discovered, over the years, that many pastors and their wives cannot resolve their call experiences. This is true for pastors, missionaries, and other ministry servants. It is hard to explain why two godly people cannot resolve the ministry calling. This does not mean one is confused and the other is not. This does not mean one has a rebellious attitude and the other does not. We will someday understand such mysteries when we stand before our Heavenly Father.

I can testify that I married a godly, supportive wife when I married Judy. She has always stood behind me in everything I do, even when it is difficult. This mission calling played itself out when we were in our early twenties. That was also the time when our two sons were born.

Judy agreed to support me if I chose to follow the mission calling. It was difficult, and we did not understand the discrepancy of our hearts, but we went in that direction.

We made application with the Foreign Mission Board of the Southern Baptist Convention. Judy was supportive of the application, but she faced health issues that were beyond her control. We had prayed for healing, but God had not seen fit to heal her of the health issues. The mission board rejected our application. That proved to be a painful and disillusioning event in my life. Did I miss God? Would God heal Judy and at some later date would we go as missionaries?

The questions I entertained were buried in the back of my mind. I did not understand, but I continued to do ministry. At the time of this writing, I have been the pastor of local churches for forty-five years. This reminds me that you may seem to strike out in one area, but you do not stop swinging.

My doubt has lingered for forty-five years. On one occasion I shared my doubt and the burden of a missed call with a pastor friend. His name is Albert. Albert once shared something that changed my life. Albert suggested that God might be doing something like He did with Abraham.

In Genesis 22, we find one of the most challenging stories recorded in the Bible. God asked Abraham to go up Mount Moriah and offer his son Isaac as a sacrifice on an altar. Abraham willingly followed God's leading. This passage has always been a challenge for believers. Questions such as: why would a loving God ask a man to offer his son as a sacrifice? Why would God ask Abraham to offer his son, whom He had promised? God said Abraham's offspring would be as the sand on the seashore. Isaac was the beginning of that promise. Had God reneged on His promise?

The rest of the story involves God bringing a resolution to the situation. Abraham carried a knife, wood for a fire, Isaac, and his faith. As Abraham was about to offer Isaac as a sacrifice, he looked up. "Abraham lifted his eyes and looked, and behold, behind him was a ram, caught in a thicket by his horns. And Abraham went and took the ram and offered it up as a burnt offering instead of his son" (Gen. 22:13-14).

This passage proved that God is good on His promises. It also teaches us that God uses those who make themselves available to His calling.

I felt totally awkward with Albert's suggestion in the previous paragraph. To his credit, he was trying to encourage a burdened pastor. Albert was not treating me as a spiritual giant, nor was he elevating me to the status of Abraham. I felt like I was walking on Holy Ground. Albert said God might be doing something "like" He did with Abraham.

We might not have it all together and may be confused, but God is always in control. We may think we made a wrong turn and missed God. This is why many people claim the promise of Romans 8:28. "And we know that for those who love God... all things work together for good" (Romans 8:28).

We find a similar idea in the book of Genesis. In a moment of jealousy, Joseph had been rejected by his brothers. His brothers sold him as a slave, resulting in him being enslaved in Egypt. While enslaved, Joseph's master's wife falsely accused Joseph of attempting to seduce her. This resulted in imprisonment.

From there, Joseph rose in power in Egypt and built the trust of the king. Joseph became one of the most powerful leaders in Egypt. It was his job to oversee the food and possessions of the king. Joseph spent many years administering the affairs of the king. In a time of famine and despair, Joseph's family went to Egypt in search of food. They stood before Joseph requesting and begging his mercy.

Joseph could have taken advantage of their helpless condition and sought revenge. He did not. Instead, he spoke these beautiful words: "And now do not be distressed or angry with yourselves because you sold me here, for God sent me before you to preserve life" (Gen. 45:5). A paraphrase of Joseph's word would be "God is in control." It is important that we understand that God is in control, even when we make wrong turns.

This chapter will help you understand why David's passing was such a traumatic experience for us. We were so proud of David. He and Erica had formed a partnership to serve Christ in a foreign country. The people of the world cannot understand this sort of pride. God's people are thrilled when they see God's work moving forward and God's people being obedient, even when it involves their family.

Judy and I felt a godly pride in our son. When he died, we struggled to process the experience. Questions such as: why a young man (41) had to die in the prime of life; why a young man had to leave behind a wife and three young children; why God would take one of His choice servants, a missionary.

It may be that you are struggling to process an experience in your life.

- For me, it was a missed call. Had I misunderstood?
- Others have struggled with similar questions, thinking they missed God. For some, it was a failed relationship. For some, it is a child that goes astray. For some, it is the failure of a business. For some, it is questions about health.

What advice can I give those who wonder if they have missed God or made a wrong turn?

The following suggestions were helpful to me.

First, when you seem to have missed God, keep working where you are. You are gifted in other areas. God works through weakness. Your confusion gives God an opportunity to work through your weakness and confusion.

Second, identify needs you can fill. Even though I did not fulfill the mission calling, I was a cheerleader for missionaries who were on the front lines. God can use wrong turns to build passion for other areas of ministry. You may not be on the front line, but you can support those who are.

Example: in the fall of 2019, I felt God leading me to provide a retreat for missionaries who were under pressure in their place of service. There was a very real possibility they were facing persecution. I had a burden to encourage and support the missionaries. I set about to raise funds to fulfill this project. We flew more than twenty missionaries from their respective country of service and conducted a four-day retreat in Thailand. This retreat was nothing heavy, just a time to have fun, relax, and relieve stress. Three months after this retreat, the missionaries were all expelled from their country. Our God saw this coming. He inspired me to act.

When you remain open to God's direction, you need not have it all together. I once preached a sermon entitled "Encouragement for Imperfect People." I used Matt. 16:13-27, as a text. In this text, we read Peter's confession of Jesus to be the "Son of God." Peter seemed to have it all together. In that same conversation, Jesus rebuked Peter because he did not understand the coming crucifixion. Peter did not have all the answers. Peter was a work in progress.

A final suggestion, *trust God.* Job once said: "Though He slay me, yet will I trust in Him." (Job 13:15). It is hard to trust God when the clouds are dark and the vision is blurred. Ultimately it boils down to trust. When I missed the mission calling, I learned to trust God. When we lost David, we had to trust God. Consider these examples:

- Trust God. In His sovereignty, He knows what is best.
- Trust God. He has a plan.
- Trust God. He is not going to throw you away because you have doubts and confusion and seem to have made a wrong turn.

One of the greatest affirmations of faith occurs when you settle the issue of God being a gracious God and trust Him. The

Psalmist said: "Oh, taste and see that the Lord is good; Blessed is the man who trusts in Him" (Ps. 34:8).

- God was gracious when the disciples missed the crucifixion.
- God was gracious when Peter denied Jesus three times.
- God was gracious when Jesus pondered why God had forsaken Him on the cross.

You might take wrong turns, make mistakes, and get confused. Rest assured; God will be there when you come out on the other side of the mountain.

FOR REFLECTION

1. Has there ever been a time when you thought you missed God or made a wrong turn?

2. What thoughts and feelings did you struggle with?

3. When the disciples, due to fear and confusion, missed the crucifixion, how do you think they felt?

Lesson 9

BELIEVERS SOMETIMES CRASH

This chapter might seem inappropriate or out of place in this book. The chapter is primarily focused on burnout. I include it for several reasons. First, many people do not understand burnout and they are disillusioned to see a minister struggling with the issue.

Second, people do not understand or feel compassion for the minister who struggles with depression and burnout. There needs to be more understanding and compassion on this subject.

Third, this chapter is a call for encouragers. One of the greatest services you can perform for others is to accept, support, and encourage them, no matter how irrational their behavior or attitude may be.

My struggle with burnout could be described as a crash. I began struggling with feelings of despair, hopelessness, and pessimism. The preaching I once enjoyed became drudgery. The visits I once loved became hectic. The people I once loved became unlovable.

Many days, I wished for a change. Another job seemed to be the answer for me.

During this period, I thought a lot about Elijah and his crisis with Jezebel (I Kings 19). Even though some may not consider Elijah's crisis burnout, his situation provided parallels to the crash I experienced.

> **AFTER CONFRONTING** the situation in my life, I was led to understand the meaning of burnout.

First, Elijah wanted to flee his problem. People surviving emotional crashes will often want to run away and hide and be by themselves. This was true of Elijah. He retreated to the wilderness (see vs. 1-4). Likewise, I wanted to get away from my pastoral duties and what I perceived to be my problem.

Elijah also felt self-pity. He thought he was the only servant of God who had remained faithful in the face of Jezebel's torture (see vs. 10). I felt self-pity which was reflected in skepticism toward others. I could not find anything good in the people I served.

Finally, Elijah was unable to win the victory of faith. He had won some great victories in the past. He had prayed for and received a three- and one-half-year drought as a source of judgment against King Ahab. He had defeated 450 prophets of Baal on one occasion. He had healed the sick and performed other miracles; however, there came a point when his faith would not serve him, let alone defeat the enemy.

After confronting the situation in my life, I was led to understand the meaning of burnout. A professional counselor helped me see that my crash was due to burnout. I was able to reach out for support during this difficult time. Where did I find support?

I was blessed to have an understanding wife. She did not fully understand my situation. She felt frustrated when I talked about other employment. However, she never scolded or criticized. She always understood as she listened to me. After therapy sessions, she was eager to hear about discussions. Even though my talk of vocational change bothered her, I always felt she supported me 100 percent. Her acceptance and understanding were critical.

Another source of support was a caring friend. He offered a reassuring ear that aided the healing process. This friend had been through a forced termination, so he knew the value of a supporting friend. His friendship and understanding were invaluable.

The greatest support during this period was a Christian psychologist who practiced near our home. He was a friend to pastors. He had invited the ministers in our association to visit his clinic and take a stress test on his new computer. I took advantage of this opportunity and discovered I had a stress problem. In the ensuing weeks, he helped me confront my stress.

I had always viewed psychologists and psychiatrists with some misgivings. I felt they were good for the emotionally and mentally ill but I had no need for them. During this period, I came to appreciate and was thankful I knew a professional psychologist. I believe every person should be acquainted with the professionals in their area. They can provide vital support.

After my encounter with burnout, I had time to reflect, discuss, and read about it. As a crisis, burnout is hard to define. Burnout victims suffer many common characteristics: pessimism, depression, loss of energy, skepticism, weight change, irregular exercise habits, and others. Considering these characteristics plus examining a person's attitude will give a clear picture of whether one is suffering from burnout.

During this burnout crisis, I came face to face with my true feelings about counselors and therapists. Along with that, I had to face my thoughts about depression. During the early phase of burnout, I struggled a lot with depression. I went to see our family doctor. He did the unthinkable. He put me on an antidepressant.

Again, I perceived antidepressants to be below my dignity. I perceived antidepressants to be something "sick" people take. I shared my hangups with the family doctor, and he quickly clarified my wrong perceptions. He compared an antidepressant to what happens when an electrical wire short circuits. He said an electrical appliance can short circuit causing a breakdown. When that occurs, we call our electrician. Once the electrician performs his magic, the appliance will be as good as new. He said the short circuit does not render the appliance unusable. The repair renders the appliance to be as good as new. My doctor told me that after taking the antidepressant for a period I would be as good as new.

In this chapter, I have discussed burnout and depression. Those were crisis-inducing experiences in my life. They caused me to crash. Was I finished? Had God tossed me away? Not on your life. God graciously provided the support I needed and got me back on my feet.

There is no sin when a believer crashes. A crash merely proves we are human and need God's amazing grace. I will discuss God's grace in chapter 10.

As I wrote this chapter, I made another wrong turn. LOL. Just for the record, I am generally good with directions. The wrong turn discussed in chapter 8 was in the Smoky Mountains. Today, it occurred in Sokol Park near our home. I often go for early morning hikes. Last week, I went on a hike in Sokol Park. As I went on that hike, I made a wrong turn and walked 1-2 miles more than planned. This week I made the same hike. I was determined not to make the same mistake again. I downloaded a trail map of the route I planned to take. I meticulously followed the trail map. I was proud of myself and my use of technology. However, the cursor pointed to the park trailhead and not to my car, which was parked in a different location.

I made another wrong turn. What is the point? I thought I could remedy my directional issue by downloading a trail map. Trail maps are wonderful tools, and we should use them. However, you can try to remedy your mistakes and prevent wrong turns, but the fact is that you are human. As you go through life, you cannot avoid all wrong turns.

It is imperative that you have a hold of God, but more importantly, that God has a hold of you. This brings us to the most important lessons in this book. You will find these in chapters 10-11.

FOR REFLECTION

1. Has there ever been a time when you crashed due to anxiety, depression, burnout, stress, or other debilitating issues?

2. Read 1 Kings 19:1-21. Can you relate to Elijah's issues: fear, self-pity, loneliness, tiredness, stress, emptiness, and feeling worthless.

3. What steps have you taken to overcome these issues?

4. Who is in your support network?

5. What steps are you taking to refresh and rekindle your spiritual fire?

Lesson 10

GOD'S AT WORK, EVEN WHEN HE SEEMS TO BE SILENT

Does it disturb you that God sometimes takes the path of silence?

- God may keep silent when storms come.
- God may keep silent when a crippling disease strikes.
- God may keep silent when injustice is apparent.
- God may keep silent when ungodliness seems to be in control.
- God may keep silent when an untimely death occurs.

Obviously, these examples are a small sampling of God's silence. For me, the challenge of God's silence would be more difficult to bear had He not allowed us to sample this reality in His word.

In Matt. 27:46, we find the agonizing prayer of Jesus as He hung on the cross. He felt forsaken by His Father. He felt the silence of Heaven.

We can never accuse God of hiding painful truth. There are many episodes in the Bible when God revealed painful truth with a sobering force.

> **WE CAN NEVER ACCUSE GOD** of hiding painful truth.

As stated in the previous paragraph, Jesus was not sheltered from the reality of God's silence. Therefore, to cope with the reality of God's silence we should learn from Jesus' experience. The Bible says Jesus cried out, "My God, My God, why have you forsaken me?" Consider these truths that come from Jesus' experience.

First, Jesus understands our struggle with God's silence. He experienced God's silence; therefore, He knows how to comfort those who have similar experiences. Silence has a way of sharpening our dependence on Jesus. He does not condemn or cast stones. He knows the agony we face during God's silence. "For we do not have a High Priest who cannot sympathize with our weaknesses, but was in all points tempted as we are, yet without sin. Let us therefore come boldly to the throne of grace, that we may obtain mercy and find grace to help in time of need" (Heb. 4:15-16).

Second, trials are not a sign of God's disfavor or lack of love. Jesus was God's beloved Son and yet God allowed Him to experience silence. If God allowed His own Son to experience His silence, despite His great love for Him, then maybe God has something in store for me.

As humans, we tend to jump to the wrong conclusions when negative things come our way. We assume God is mad at us or that He does not love us. Jesus' experience negates this foregone conclusion.

Third, God often does His greatest work when He seems to be silent. God appeared to be silent as Jesus hung on the cross. However, after three days, God's sovereignty displayed itself as He raised Jesus from the grave. God performed the greatest miracle in the history of the world.

The popular piece "Footprints in the Sand" illustrates God's unseen work, when He seems to be silent. The struggler in this story complains and blames God because there was only one set of footprints in the sand when life got tough. He assumed God had forsaken him. However, the struggler quickly learns that the one set of prints does not indicate God's absence during times of trouble. Rather, the one set of prints represents the sustaining presence of God during life's trying times. God carries us during trying times. God may seem to be absent during various seasons of our life. That is not the case. During those times His sustaining presence has a greater work to fulfill.[i]

God is at work, even when He seems to be silent. There have been several occasions in our family life when God seemed to be silent. In those moments, we discovered God to be sovereign, in control, and actively working. In this chapter, I defer to two family members. Their stories beautifully illustrate God's sovereign control, even though He seemed to be silent.

JUDY

My wife Judy has been my friend, helper, and support for forty-five years at the time of this writing. There is much I could say about her as a mate. However, the thing I wish to highlight is the sovereign work of God in her life. Much of that work occurred in spite of God seeming to be silent.

Judy is the Executive Director of the New Day Women's Center in Tuscaloosa County, Alabama. She was hired to be the Executive Director of Save-a-Life, of Tuscaloosa County. The overturn of *Roe vs. Wade* resulted in the restructuring of Save-a-Life to become New Day Women's Center.

It is amazing how Judy came to be the Executive Director of this wonderful organization. I am constantly telling people that God has been preparing Judy all her life for this position. She is a walking miracle.

Her preparation began at birth. Judy's birth was a difficult birth. She was born face first. Her face was disfigured from the long birthing journey. The cord was wrapped around her neck, and she was turning blue. The medical staff said the baby looked like a Mongaloid (today we call such a baby a Down Syndrome baby). Judy's mother's oldest sister was a nurse and in the delivery room that day. That night she went home and told the family, "I hope the baby dies because there's something wrong with her." In the hospital, Judy's mother had a roommate. When the roommate's mother came to visit, she would look at Judy's mother and say, "Oh honey, if you raise this baby, you will have a hard life."

Judy's mother was in despair. One day another nurse walked into the mother's room and saw her crying as she held her baby. The nurse walked to her bedside and said, "Oh, honey, it's going to be OK. Let me show you what you can do to help reshape her face." The nurse continued to comfort Judy's mother. She didn't have all the answers or solutions, but she did share hope with Judy's mother.

Even in birth God was not silent. He was at work. You can see the sovereign development of a lady who would be an advocate for the unborn. The Bible says: "we are fearfully and wonderfully made (Ps. 139:14).

From the time we are conceived in the womb, God is preparing us for His service. It was said of the prophet Jeremiah: "Before I formed you in the womb, I knew you; and before you were born,

I consecrated you; I appointed you a prophet unto the nations" (Jer. 1:5). God was in control.

The next illustration of God's sovereignty showed itself when babies started coming into our family. We had two sons. After the birth of our second son, Judy suffered post-partem depression. The post-partem depression grew into full blown depression. For Judy, depression had a travelling companion, anxiety.

The depression and anxiety caused Judy to miss many life enjoyments and retreat into a shell. Her anxiety caused her to avoid open places and people. This was not the ideal trait for a pastor's wife.

On one occasion, a church I was serving planned a mission trip to northwest Montana. Judy and I decided to drive to Montana and on the way stop by Mount Rushmore. We both expected that stop. However, when we arrived at Mount Rushmore Judy was a prisoner in our car. She could not bring herself to leave the security of the car, no matter the appeal of Mount Rushmore.

Judy was determined, despite the depression and anxiety. She fought these two enemies with relentless courage. Also, she once prayed: "Lord, if you will heal me of this problem, I would like to dedicate the remainder of my life to helping women who struggle with similar issues."

From the depression/anxiety struggle, you can see God raising a servant who has a heart for supporting others. Special note: many ladies who have faced the issues associated with childbearing need someone who understands.

Another evidence of God's sovereign work came in women's ministry. In the years leading up to the New Day position, Judy worked extensively with women's ministry in local churches. In fact, she was one of the first ladies to earn a Doctorate in the Southern Baptist Convention, specializing in women's ministry. The doctorate would later strengthen her resume for the New Day position.

Her involvement in women's ministry earned the respect of leaders of the Louisiana Baptist Convention. The convention undertook a consolidation of WMU (Woman's Missionary Union) and the state's women's ministry. Judy was selected to chair that statewide initiative.

God's sovereign involvement was evident in Judy's birth, depression, and rise to become a leader in women's ministry activities. These are just some of the ways God's sovereignty prepared her to be the Executive Director of New Day. God was not silent.

Her leadership of New Day has been blessed. Their budget has doubled. Many contributors and supporters have stepped up to expand the ministry. The staff has expanded. They have bought a new building, thus expanding the potential of the ministry.

I am reminded of the Old Testament character Esther. Esther's uncle Mordecai once told her God had placed her "for such a time as this" (Esther 4:14). I feel as if God has been preparing Judy for such a time as this.

I find this to be particularly intriguing because of the life phase Judy and I are facing. We are facing a time when we will ride off into the sunset of retirement. However, God chose to raise her up for this special opportunity, despite this phase of life.

DAVID

The second story of God's seeming silence occurred with the passing of our oldest son David. This book is dedicated to his memory.

We struggled with the emotion of this experience. However, in the days that followed it became obvious that David's death was in the sovereign plan of God. God was not silent. Was that easy to accept? Not at all. One of the hardest things for a believer to accept is God's sovereignty. Job once said: "Though he slay me, yet will I trust in Him" (Job 13:15). Job also said: "The Lord gave, and the Lord has taken away; blessed be the name of the Lord" (Job 1:21).

The following article, written by Judy, states our feelings perfectly.

A mother's resolve: God is sovereign, faithful, and loving. By Judy Patrick[ii]

ALEXANDRIA, La. (LBM) -- Oct. 14, 2020, will be ingrained in my mind forever. Around 7 o'clock that morning, my daughter-in-law called my husband to tell us that our 41-year-old son had died suddenly from an apparent cardiac arrhythmia.

We were in shock.

David had no history of heart issues. He was disciplined to watch what he ate and to exercise regularly. He was a very slim and fit young man. Just a week earlier, he had passed his annual physical with flying colors.

How does a parent wrap her mind around such news?

My first reactions were: "I didn't get to tell him goodbye. I didn't get to see him one last time. Did my child suffer? Did he die in pain?"

But the thoughts that have carried me through this horrific crisis have been: "God is sovereign. God is faithful. And God is loving."

At first, I simply repeated these three phrases over and over in my head.

But after a few weeks, I began to ask myself, "What do you really believe about these three statements? What is it about these three declarations that sustains you?"

Truly, the loss of my son was a crisis of belief for me.

Before I go any further, I need to share a few details about David's life in the months prior to his death.

David and his wife Erica had been missionaries in East Asia for 16 years. Eight months before he died, he, she, and their children (ages six, nine, and 11) had been in lockdown because of COVID-19. Shortly after release from quarantine, they were told to leave their beloved mission field and they were given three days to pack what they could in 15 luggage bags (three each).

Fifteen bags is not much in comparison to all they had to leave behind ... furniture, appliances, toys, vehicles, kitchen wares, books, etc.

They were sent to Thailand until further notice and placed in lockdown, again because of the novel

Coronavirus. Then, after two months of quarantine, the family finally was permitted to fly to the United States.

They arrived stateside in May and received word about a new assignment to Taiwan. But from then until October the family anxiously waited to get back on the mission field while updating passports, applying for visas and obtaining permission to enter the country despite the pandemic. Additionally, David and Erica were told to put together a team to do strategic work among pastors in Taiwan. Meanwhile, David used his time here to speak at churches.

By the end of September, David had his team and all that was left to do was follow up on the family's visas.

Losing their home, possessions, dreams, friends, and all he and Erica had worked to accomplish in 16 years was devastating. But now things were looking up. They were sitting on "GO." And then Oct. 14 happened.

So, back to the beginning of my story. God is sovereign. God is faithful. And God is loving.

God is sovereign. So, what am I supposed to do with that? I can't escape anything God wants to dish out. God is all-knowing, all-seeing, everywhere all the time. God has always been and will always be. God is in control of EVERYTHING. Where do I find resolve in such?

I've read the book of Job and I know that what God told Job should apply to me as well. But losing MY SON was very personal.

Who am I to say to the Lord, "This isn't fair, Lord. What are You thinking? David was serving you faithfully. WHY?"

When my two sons were little, it seemed that their middle names were "Why".

"Why can't I...? Why won't you let me...? Why is...?" So many "why" questions.

As a mother, if I felt my children were mature enough to understand "why," then I told them. However, often, I simply said, "Because I'm your mother, and I say so."

In a sense, as a parent, I, too, was sovereign over my young children. I knew things they were not yet able to comprehend. I had authority over them and was responsible for their well-being. Therefore, I did not always offer reasons to them for my decisions.

Often, we respond to God much like our children respond to us with the "why" question.

What I am learning is that accepting the sovereignty of God begins with realizing He knows what we do not understand. God sees what we cannot see, and God does for us what needs to be done to shape us into the person He created us to be. God is focused on the here and now in context of His eternity.

God is faithful. To be faithful is to be loyal and constant...true to one's word.

God's actions are consistent with His character. Romans

8:28 (NIV) says: "And we know that in all things God works for the good of those who love Him, who have been called according to His purpose."

From the moment I learned of David's death, I have witnessed God's faithfulness. At the time, he and his family were living in a mission home next door to the hosting church. That morning, a deacon of the congregation was having his quiet time when he felt compelled to go to the church (around 6:00 a.m.). He arrived just seconds after Erica had found David on the ground where he had been exercising. God provided support for Erica in such a timely manner.

As you can imagine, Erica was distraught over the death of her husband. She had lost the love of her life and her ministry partner as well. Erica was committed to missions in East Asia before meeting David. He too was called to share Christ in East Asia. They were in love with each other, and they were in love with East Asians, committed to sharing God's love with them.

Now what was Erica to do?
She could no longer go to her beloved country in East Asia. Her husband was gone. She was now a single mother to three young children. How would she provide for her family? Where would she go? What would she do?

Again, God was faithful.

As a missionary for the Southern Baptist Convention, Erica was given bereavement leave with full pay for 12 months. Additionally, the International Mission Board promised her a job when she was ready to get back on the field. On top of that backdrop of needs met, people from all around the world have reached out to Erica and the children with financial and prayer support.

It has been amazing to watch God provide "for good, for those who are called according to His purpose." (Romans 8:28)

God's faithfulness goes even deeper than what we see outwardly. He knows the mental, emotional, and spiritual needs of one in such great loss.

It is in times like this, when anyone can waver that God, in His tender mercy, provided just the right people to walk with Erica, holding her up when she did not have the strength to stand on her own.

God provided a godly counselor to walk with Erica. They met weekly. Each week I've seen Erica's faith grow stronger and stronger. I've seen her emotional stability grounded in her faith. Erica has firmly accepted what God ordained from the beginning.

Yes, losing David has been painful.

Yes, it will be lonely doing missions without her beloved husband.

And yes, single parenting will have its challenges.
But God has provided a strong Christian support system for Erica to lean on. Erica has found confidence in God because of His faithfulness.

God is love. WOW. Is this what God's love looks like? A mother losing her eldest son when he's in the prime of his life; a young woman being widowed with three children not even half grown; and, three young children being left fatherless is this what God's love looks like?

No, this is what life in a fallen world looks like. This is reality for some. Not everyone will experience this kind of pain. But for those that do, this is NOT God's expression of love.

Throughout Scripture, God proclaims His love for us (NIV):

-- Isaiah 54:10: "Though the mountains be shaken, and the hills be removed, yet my unfailing love for you will not be shaken nor my covenant of peace be removed, says the Lord, who has compassion on you." Our world may be shaken to the core, but God's love will never abandon us.

-- Psalm 136:26: "Give thanks to the God of Heaven. His love endures forever."

-- Psalm 86:15: "But you, Lord, are a compassionate and gracious God, slow to anger, abounding in love and faithfulness."

-- 1 John 3:1: "See what great love the Father has lavished on us, that we should be called children of God. And that is what we are."

-- 1 John 4:9-11: "This is how God showed His love among us: He sent His one and only Son into the world that we might live through Him. This is love: not that we loved God, but that He loved us and sent His Son as an atoning sacrifice for our sins. Dear friends, since God so loved us, we also ought to love one another."

These verses remind me that we did not become God's children at no expense to Him. It cost our Father dearly to bring humankind into His family. But I am reminded also that God's love endures forever.

So how do I find resolve in the death of my son by looking to God's sovereignty, faithfulness, and love?

Because of God's sovereignty, I find strength in His power. I trust His faithfulness because He has been dependable for all generations. And, most importantly, He demonstrated His love by the sacrifice of His Son, Jesus Christ.

-- Judy Patrick

> "Know therefore that the Lord your God is God; He is the faithful God, keeping His covenant of love to a thousand generations of those who love Him and keep His commandments" Deuteronomy 7:9 (NIV).

Judy's article summarizes our confidence in God's sovereignty, faithfulness, and love. In the days that followed David's passing, God's sovereignty was on display in other ways. Judy mentioned the deacon who showed up as Erica found David lying unconscious on the ground.

God's sovereignty was on display using technology. David's family was living in a mission home at Five Points Baptist Church in Northport, Alabama. After his death, many questions were on people's mind. The pastor at Five Points checked the church's security camera to see if it held any clues. Sure enough, the security camera showed a six- or seven-minute sequence leading up to David's death. The security camera does not confirm God's sovereignty in this event. However, the following picture speaks volumes.

The last thing David did was raise his hands toward Heaven. That picture has provided tremendous comfort to Judy and me. We feel David knew what was happening and resigned himself to the Father's will.

One further evidence of God's sovereign work came at the hands of fellow missionaries. In May, before his death in October, David asked several young missionary associates to write an overview of his life. This exercise could be described as preparing an obituary. His goal was to encourage the missionaries to see life from the end, rather than the beginning. We tend to live life in the present tense. We focus on the here and now, rather than on eternity. However, as believers, life is about eternity.

The Bible says: "God so loved the world, that He gave His only Son that whoever believes in Him, should not perish but have eternal life" (John 3:16). That is the important truth we proclaim.

At David's funeral, the obituary was prepared. The mission associates had the exercise from May in their hands. Several of them stood at David's funeral and comforted our family with their kind words.

A church custodian, a video recording, and fellow missionaries were evidence of God's sovereign presence. There are always question marks when God works His plan. As we travel through life, there will always be situations we do not understand. Those situations will be shadowed by a question mark. Those of us who live by faith may have doubts, but we have the inner assurance that God has a plan, and He is at work.

Lesson 11

GOD'S GRACE WILL CARRY YOU

One of the all-time favorite hymns of the Christian faith is *AMAZING GRACE*. People have sung it in church, listened to it at funerals, and celebrated its words on special occasions. What strikes me is the way the song follows the progression of your faith development. God's grace follows you in every phase of life. Verse one highlights God's grace in conversion, "I once was lost, but now am found". Verse two highlights God's grace as we face fear, "And grace my fears relieved". Verse three highlights God's grace as we face trials, "Through many dangers, toils, and snares, I have already come". The latter part of the song highlights God's promise of Heaven, "But God, who called me here below, Will be forever mine".

As I look back on my life, I discovered the only reason God called me to ministry, and the reason I survived, was God's grace and mercy. We serve a gracious God.

Be reminded why God's grace (mercy) is so essential to us finishing our journey in this world. **God's grace and mercy are**

essential to our eternal destiny. The Bible teaches that God is a Holy, righteous God. A quick look in the mirror reminds us that we fall short of that lofty standard. The Bible says: "All have sinned and come short of the glory of God" (Romans 3:23). Our imperfection and sin keep us from enjoying and establishing a relationship with the Holy God of Heaven. Because of His grace and mercy, we can approach Him and develop a personal relationship with Him.

Not only does God allow and invite a personal relationship, but He also tolerates our imperfections. Throughout the Bible we see believers who succeeded in spite of themselves.

- Jacob was the original J.R. Ewing of the Bible. For younger people, J.R. Ewing was a character on the television series Dallas. He was guilty of manipulation, scheming, and doing whatever it took to get ahead (Gen. 27-35).
- Abraham was guilty of lying, to save himself, when he got in a jam (Gen. 12:10-20; 20:1-18).
- Peter was guilty of denying Jesus three times as Jesus moved toward the cross (Matt. 26:31—75).

These references illustrate that, God uses imperfect people. Even after we embrace faith in God, we are not perfect. I recall several times when God's grace carried me. Consider these examples.

When He called me to the gospel ministry, he was gracious. When He called, I ran the opposite direction. He called me when I was sixteen. I rebelled until I was twenty-one. His patience sustained me during that period.

He could have forcefully pushed me to do His will, but He did not. He graciously appealed to my heart. I tried to bargain with Him. Thoughts punctuated my mind: "God I will be a good layperson in my church." I tried to formulate an alternative plan.

Bargaining and alternative plans did not work. He was firm and persistent, but also gracious and loving.

The greatest influence in my life during those five years was Cindy, the girlfriend. She was enthusiastic, positive, and cheerful about faith. She was a gift of God's grace. Those traits appealed to me, even when I was not looking to do God's will.

Another expression of God's grace occurred when I misinterpreted God's will. There have been times when I missed God's will (see chapter 7). However, one incident stands out. When I was in my mid-twenties, I served a church in rural Mississippi. I was a Louisiana native, so I assumed I would one day return to my home state. I did not put that before God's will, but it was a natural assumption.

We have comfort zones into which we settle. Our home is one of those. There is not a right or wrong place where we should live. We tend to live in places with which we are familiar. Thus, the opportunity to return to my home state appealed to me. I had no problem with Mississippi.

A church from northeast Louisiana contacted me about becoming their pastor. The Mississippi church was my first church out of seminary. It was not large enough to support our family. The appeal of Louisiana and the size of the church caused me to make a hasty decision. I did not pray and wait on God. I made a wrong decision about God's will.

I resigned from the Mississippi church on a Wednesday night and notified the Louisiana church I would be accepting their call. I immediately knew I had made the wrong decision.

God was gracious with me. I ended up staying in the Mississippi church for another two years. I was humiliated by that experience, but God was gracious.

Another instance of God's grace occurred on one of the occasions when I stumbled. I stumbled when I experienced burnout. This was discussed extensively in the previous chapter.

God's grace encourages, enriches, and strengthens us for ministry. Consider the example of Gideon. Gideon was called to lead the Israelite people out of bondage to the Midianites. Gideon was a reluctant leader. He doubted God's goodness. He said: "Why then has all this happened to us?" (vs. 13).

He doubted God's presence. He said: "the Lord has forsaken us" (vs. 13). He doubted himself. He said: "O my Lord, how can I save Israel? Indeed, my clan is the weakest in Manasseh, and I am the least in my father's house" (vs. 15).

In addition to the doubt Gideon asked for a sign and threw a fleece to verify God's call. He said: "If You will save Israel by my hand as You have said look, I shall put a fleece of wool on the threshing floor" (vs. 36-37). He asked for an answer as he lay the fleece on the ground. This happened twice. He asked that it lay on the ground overnight. One time he prayed that the fleece would be dry in the morning. One time he prayed that the fleece would be wet in the morning. These two episodes were merely extensions of his doubt.

Despite Gideon's flaws, God used him. "Thus, Midian was subdued before the children of Israel so that they lifted their heads no more. And the country was quiet for forty years in the days of Gideon (Judges 8:28)." I believe you would agree, God showed grace with Gideon.

Since the day I accepted Christ as my Savior and the day I entered the ministry, God has been gracious to me. Have we not all experienced God's grace in so many ways? We doubt Him. We fail Him.

I remember an occasion when God clearly instructed me to share a word of faith with a gentleman. I had finished a visit at a local hospital and was in a hurry. The man was standing at the door of the hospital. I passed him by. My hurry caused me to miss God's appointment that day.

It has been a challenge for me to implement the truth I observed in John 4. In that chapter Jesus detours through Samaria. The Bible says: "He had to pass through Samaria" (John 4:4). Jesus was never hurried or bothered by interruptions. He interrupted his busy schedule to minister to a lady in Samaria who needed a visit from Him.

When I bypassed the man at the hospital, I was clearly mission driven. The sad part was that I did not take the time to be Jesus to that man. This example is one example from my life. All of you have experiences when you missed God or disobeyed a clear command. I am not looking to magnify our failures. I am looking to magnify the marvelous grace of God.

As you read this book, you observed a few occasions when God moved in dramatic ways in my life. It was dramatic when I helped the woman on the way to New Orleans. That episode was the inspiration for the book. It was dramatic when God called me to be a pastor. It was dramatic when the church voted on the staff member and I recorded the affirmative vote before it occurred. I could have included other experiences. The experiences I shared were for illustrative purposes, not to gloat over my spiritual accomplishments. For some mysterious reason *God chose to display His grace* through these dramatic experiences.

I have shared experiences when I made wrong turns and some when I crashed, due to burnout or depression. I could not have survived the past forty-six years of ministry apart from the grace of God. As Jesus taught His disciples, He emphasized that He would "keep" them (John 17:11-15). He is still keeping His children. I have succeeded because Jesus has "kept" me. His grace is sufficient.

The Good News is this: "God's grace will carry you." A major lesson I have learned is that we serve a gracious God.

There is always a new day coming. The Bible says: "His compassions are new every morning" (Lam. 3:23). Hang in there, God will show up.

FOR REFLECTION

1. Has there been a time/times in your life when you clearly did not fulfill God's plans. Share this with someone.

2. Did you confess the failure to God?

3. What did you do to move beyond your failure and walk in the goodness of God's grace?

About the Author

Pastor Tim (as he prefers to be called) has served as a pastor since his early twenties. He turned seventy as this book was being completed. Pastor Tim served churches in Louisiana, Mississippi, Florida, and Alabama. He and Judy, his wife, currently live in Adairsville, Georgia, where they are partially retired and serve as hospice chaplains with HomeSpun Hospice.

ENDNOTE

[i] *Footprints in the Sand,* Authorship undetermined.

[ii] Permission to reprint article in Chapter 10, p. 72, granted by The Baptist Messenger, 2024.

Made in the USA
Columbia, SC
31 July 2024